Speed

BILL ALLEN

Trap

Bill Allen, 2007

EIGHTY ROBBERIES
AND FIFTY YEARS

Speed

BILL ALLEN

Trap

Parkhurst Brothers, Inc., Publishers
LITTLE ROCK

www.parkhurstbrothers.com

Parkhurst Brothers books and e-books are distributed to the trade through the Chicago Distribution Center, a unit of the University of Chicago Press, and may be ordered through Ingram Book Company, Baker & Taylor, Follett Library Resources and other book industry wholesalers. To order from the University of Chicago's Chicago Distribution Center, phone 1-800-621-2736 or send a fax to 1-800-621-8476. Copies of this and other Parkhurst Brothers, Inc., Publishers titles are available to organizations and corporations for purchase in quantity by contacting Special Sales Department at our home office location, listed on our web site.

Printed in the United States of America
First Edition, 2012

2010 2011 2012 2013 2014 2015 2016   12 11 10 9 8 7 6 5 4 3 2 1

Library of Congress Control Number: 2009942597

ISBN: original trade paperback   978-1-935166-23-8 [10 digit: 1-935166-23-9]
ISBN: e-book   978-1-935166-83-2 [10-digit: 1-935166-83-2]

Design Director and Cover Design:
Wendell E. Hall

Page design:
Shelly Culbertson

Acquired for Parkhurst Brothers, Inc., Publishers by:
Ted Parkhurst

Editor:
Sandie Williams

112012

Dedication and Acknowledgements

This work is dedicated to my mother,
whose unconditional love never waned or wavered.

I would like to thank Bill and Ruby Hill. Their
encouragement, prayers and proofreading skills helped make
this book possible. I would also like to thank Lynne Rowland
who suggested that my publisher read my manuscript.
Last but certainly not least, I would like to thank my family
who I caused to suffer simply because they loved me.

Table of Contents

*Bill and Debbie Allen
at their wedding, April 2012*

Bill and Debbie on honeymoon, 2012

Drugs Taken
At Pharmacy

A man armed with 45-caliber revolver robbed the Blake Pharmacy at 175 West Sixty-fifth Street of an undetermined amount of drugs about 5:36 p.m. Monday, a police spokesman said. Andy M. Stoner, the stores operator, told officers the man, smelling of alcohol, entered the store with the gun and ordered him to hand over all the store's "Schedule 2" controlled drugs. Many of which contain narcotic. Stoner and two other employees then gave the man some drugs and he left without taking any money. The store employees were unable to determine the amount of drugs taken Monday.

ARKANSAS GAZETTE,
Tuesday. Jan.1, 1980   11A

CHAPTER ONE

A Man with a Gun

Under heaven all can see beauty as beauty
only because there is ugliness.
All can know good as good only because there is evil.

—LAO TZU

"This is a forty-five automatic, capable of killing every damn one of you!"

I was in my element, standing behind the prescription counter of Blake Pharmacy, toting a big pistol, a bigger habit, and a bad attitude.

First, I pointed the pistol at a teenaged girl who wore her long dark hair twisted into a single braid and was operating the front register, then at a middle-aged male customer making a purchase at her counter. I demanded, "Get your butts back here right now!"

The pharmacy area was on a six-inch raised platform which afforded me a panoramic view of the store. It also provided the clerk and customer a clear view of the masked gunman screaming at them. Both turned abruptly at my command, noticing me for the first time. I was not an intimidating sight without the forty-five and ski mask. Twenty-three years old, standing only five feet nine inches in my socks, I strained to tip the scales at one hundred and sixty-five pounds. Teenage acne still spotted my jaw line, and nobody would confuse me with Arnold Schwarzenegger.

The girl, a pretty little thing, with sparkling eyes and shining hair any man would love to see splayed over a pillowcase, won my sympathy in her fright. She immediately acquiesced. The man—probably a highway engineer judging by the number of ball-point pens clipped to his shirt pocket—hesitated, looking for somewhere to flee. Uncertainty and fear competed for supremacy in his face. Looking from me to the front door and then back again, he gauged the distance between himself and me and the distance to the front door, calculating whether he could make it out the door before I sent 260 grains of lead at 3,500 feet per second crashing through his skull.

"Don't try it, or I'll blow your head off!" I screamed. I had no mercy for the male victims of my robberies. Enjoying the intimidation the gun provided, I projected as threatening an image as I could muster.

Apparently, he believed me. His shoulders slumped as compliance supplanted fear and indecision. Slowly, he walked toward me. The girl reached my elevated vantage point behind the counter first. In a soft voice, I directed her to lie on the floor. Next, the man approached, and I said, "Smart move buddy. You'll live another day." With a wave of my pistol, I then indicated that he should accompany the girl onto the floor.

A quick survey of the pharmacy exposed no other potential threats. Blake Pharmacy, a typical neighborhood drug store located in a small shopping center on the corner of Sixty-Fifth Street and Blake Drive in Little Rock, Arkansas, was under my command. I could see people walking to and from their cars in the parking lot through the big glass windows that comprised the storefront. They were of no concern. My victims and I were alone. Only ointments, medicines and my captives' fears witnessed my felony.

The pharmacist, a gray-haired man in his mid fifties, stood mute beside me, visibly frightened. He shook so much it appeared he might collapse from a coronary. However, I was not concerned about his dying on me; I knew he was simply the shaky type. You see, I had been here before. This was my second trip to Blake Pharmacy in four years. The first time, I was certain he would keel over dead before I escaped with the drugs I sought. My concern had been unfounded; he cooperated with me completely and lived to report the event to the police.

A year after that first encounter at Blake I was arrested for a different pharmacy holdup. At that time, the police placed me in lineups for every unsolved drug store robbery in Little Rock. The detective in charge of the investigation, David Chapel, had asked me, "Bill Allen, why is Mr. Stoner so frightened of you?"

Chapel told me about attempting to get the pharmacist, Mr. Stoner, to view the lineup in hopes he could charge me with that robbery, too. Stoner told the police, "Let him go! Send him to prison! Do whatever you want with him, but I'm not coming near him for any reason!"

Not a good decision on his part. Had he viewed that lineup, he probably would have identified me. I didn't wear a mask that first time. Identifying me could have solved this crime and prevented the ones to come.

With the customers under control and the pharmacist awaiting instruction, I took a moment to indulge in the high of power that comes with armed robbery.

I would not even admit it to myself at the time, but I now believe I robbed pharmacies as much for the perverse feeling of dominance as I did for the drugs. The total control of people, the ability to pass any judgment, commit any atrocity against them, was a thrill that knew no greater feeling.. There is unquestionable truth in the dictum, "Absolute power corrupts absolutely."

Yet, dope is the commodity for which I had come, and it was time to get on

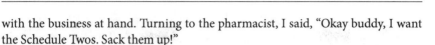

with the business at hand. Turning to the pharmacist, I said, "Okay buddy, I want the Schedule Twos. Sack them up!"

I handed him the white pillowcase I had stripped from my pillow at home. Without hesitation, he turned to the shelves lining the back of the pharmacy area that were full of pill bottles. There were three separate sections making up the dope shelf. Each section was shaped like a U turned on its side with the opening facing the front of the store.

The frightened pharmacist walked directly to the back of the center section and knelt on the floor. He proceeded to rake all of the bottles from the bottom shelf and then lifted up the shelf itself revealing a hidden compartment where all the good dope was stashed.

Taking my pillowcase in his right hand, he inserted his left arm in the compartment and started "sacking them up," per my orders. When he had placed the last bottle of pills in the pillowcase, he attempted to stand and return it to me. I had been here before though, and, the last time I robbed this store, the pharmacist had revealed an identical compartment on the left hand side of this section.

"Nice try buddy," I told him, "Now open the other hidden compartment and give me those drugs, too. You'd better get it all this time. If I find out that you are holding out on me, it will be your final mistake."

Not having time to contemplate his error, he complied, filling my pillowcase past halfway and making a very happy man out of one aggravated robber. Relieving him of his burden, I instructed him to open the back door. He rose as quickly as his trembling would allow. By the fleeting, grateful expression on his face, it was obvious he hoped I was preparing to leave and this mid-afternoon nightmare would finally come to an end. Suddenly the expression on his face betrayed the realization that if I planned to kill him, now was the time I would do it. He searched my eyes, trying to discern my intent through the narrow slits of the mask. I told him, more to prevent him from trying anything stupid than in an effort to reassure him, that if he continued to behave, he would live.

As we walked past the clerk and customer lying on the floor, I directed one last set of instructions to them, "I'm going to leave and nobody has been hurt. But if you move *one muscle* before I get out of here, I swear I'll kill you."

Convinced they would cause no trouble, I followed the pharmacist into the small back room that served as a storage area. Boxes were stacked haphazardly against the right-hand wall. On the left was an employees' restroom, the door wide open. A ten-speed bicycle, which I suspected belonged to the attractive female employee, rested on its kickstand in the middle of the room. The pharmacist walked around the bike to the metal service door and, after a few seconds, managed to overcome the shakes long enough to insert the key.

"Just open it a crack and then backup," I said, no longer screaming, no longer enjoying the power. I was just ready to get out of there with my dope.

Removing the key from the door, the pharmacist complied and I shoved him inside the restroom. "Lie on the floor and shut the door. Don't come out until you're sure I am miles away. If I see you again, you are a *dead man.*" This last command, issued with such calm assurance, sounded ominous even to my calloused ears.

I wasted no time as the bathroom door swung shut. Jerking the ski mask from my head and being careful not to touch the door with my ungloved hand, I opened it and peeked outside. The bright winter sun's glare forced me to squint as I scanned the area. Failing to find cause for concern, I plunged the gun down the front of my pants—not recommended with a loaded and cocked forty-five automatic—and slipped out the door. Walking swiftly, but not rapidly enough to draw attention, I crossed a narrow alley and passed through a gate in a chain-link fence that separated the shopping center from an apartment complex. I rounded the corner of the first apartment building and spotted my driver, Henry Small, sitting in his old scraped, once-shiny blue Buick, waiting where I had instructed him to park.

I jumped into the car and slammed the door. Henry just sat there looking at the sack of drugs as if he could not comprehend how I had acquired it. "Get out of here!" I demanded. This brought Henry around, and he started the car. The aged V-8 cried out in a cacophony of ill repair, causing me to doubt the Buick's ability to deliver us from the crime scene. Henry drove out of the apartment complex and turned right on Blake Drive, with about a half-mile of residential neighborhood to drive through before turning north on I-30. Freshly-painted two and three bedroom houses built a generation or two earlier alternated with overgrown yards with penned or chained dogs and old Chevrolets rusting beside empty carports.

As the Buick entered the flow of traffic on the interstate, I pulled the pistol from my pants and turned towards Henry. Holding the gun low, so that no passing motorist could see it, I pointed it at him and bobbled the barrel for effect. In my most ominous voice, I said, "Henry, I have seven rounds in this clip and one in the chamber. *Do not stop* for any reason. If the cops get behind us, you better do your best to outrun them. Believe me when I tell you, *buddy,* I have six bullets for the police, one for you, and one for me. If at any point you attempt to pull over, you'll get yours first!"

Henry later took offense at this clear threat, but the was not about to take issue as long as the forty-five was pointed at his belly. The drive out of Little Rock was uneventful. We did see two Little Rock city police cars traveling south on I-30, their blue lights flashing, but that was all. We crossed the Arkansas River, which brought us to North Little Rock, then commuted with the light traffic for about a mile and a half east on I-40. As we approached the Lakewood exit, the lakeside upper middle class suburb where I spent my youth, I noticed an Arkansas State Trooper virtually hidden in the deep shadow of the overpass.

"Just keep it under sixty," I cautioned Henry as we drove past.

I was skeptical of my driver. This was his first time to drive for me so I kept him under close scrutiny. Henry and I met in 1977 at the Benton Work Release Center of the Arkansas Department of Correction, a half-way unit thirty miles southwest of Little Rock. Since his release, Henry had lost the lower part of his left leg due to a gangrene infection resulting from shooting homemade bathtub crank into an artery in his foot with a less-than-sterile syringe. Poor Henry was no longer fleet of foot. Unsuited for many crimes, he had jumped at the opportunity to be my driver. The one thing I really liked about Henry was that he knew when to be quiet. I am not the type of person who appreciates unnecessary conversation, and Henry understood. It is a good thing, too, because Henry had one of those squeaky voices that can get on my nerves. When he talked, he ended every sentence with a wheezing exhale which left me wondering if he had finished talking or was simply out of breath.

With the trooper out of sight, we turned north on 67-167 and proceeded past McCain Mall. I chuckled quietly to myself as we passed the mall. Memories from my youth, of parties held in the woods where the mall now stands, flooded my mind. Those phantom woods had been the scene of many youthful parties, my buddies and I drinking Boone's Farm Strawberry Hill wine, smoking dope, boasting around the campfire of our past sexual conquests and occasionally achieving a new one. Pushing those fond memories aside, I continued watching the road ahead and behind us. It was not yet time to relax or entertain frivolous thoughts. We had just committed a crime that could net each of us a life sentence and—in the State of Arkansas—life means *life*.

As we entered the city limits of Sherwood, we drove past my ex-bosses, Ned Barker and Fred Hastings loading a boat trailer at Concord Boats. I had recently quit my job at Concord and did not allow myself to reflect on it or them. My inability to keep the job revealed a character weakness that I was not ready to admit—even to myself. The holdup today was my first robbery since being released from prison on December 1, 1978, and was the beginning of a treacherous slide that would continue until I effectively made a total and irreparable wreck of my life.

Henry turned off the highway at the Sherwood exit and drove the short distance to Indian Cove Apartments where we shared a townhouse. Since we were both on parole, our living together constituted a violation. However, aggravated robbery being a much more serious infraction, our joint residence distressed neither of us.

Indian Cove Apartments was a complex of eight brick buildings. In each building were three 2-story apartments. Parking in front of our apartment, Henry slowly climbed from the car and unlocked the front door. After stuffing the gun back down the front of my pants and making sure no nosy neighbors were observing, I slid out of the car with the bulging pillow case, our booty. The pills rattled loudly in their bottles as I hurried to get inside the apartment.

After I shut the apartment door, Henry, excited by our successful venture, grabbed me in a bear hug and exclaimed, "We did it!" Releasing me, he asked, "What all did we get?"

"I don't know. Let's go upstairs and see."

Henry followed me up the narrow stairs and into his bedroom. We selected this room because it was located at the front of the apartment with a window overlooking the parking lot. His walls were thumb-tacked full of cheap posters: rock-n-roll groups brandishing their guitars like AK-47s. I walked to the window, pulled the dark blue curtains aside, and took a quick survey to assure myself that no law enforcement officers were besieging our humble abode. No cops were in sight, so I proceeded to my second-favorite part of pharmacy robberies. Grasping the bottom of the pillowcase, I dumped all of the pill bottles onto Henry's bargain waterbed, the type that threatens to toss you onto the floor every time you move.

"Wow!" exclaimed Henry as his eyes bulged at the sight of our haul. "Man, we're rich!"

We carefully sat on his bed and commenced examining our take. "All right! Preluden 75s," I declared as I spotted the familiar orange pills.

"Here's some 50s too," I said, holding up a bottle of large white, yet significantly weaker, Preluden.

"Dilaudid! They are only K2s though. And here's some quarter grain morphine," I continued our inventory, disappointed that the Dilaudid was not four milligrams. I would have been much happier if the morphine had been the stronger half grains, but I was still gratified to find these big money drugs in our stash.

"I don't see any Desoxyn. Damn it, Bill. There isn't any Desoxyn."

Henry and I were speed freaks. Preluden and Desoxyn were our drugs of choice.

Preluden had changed since the early seventies when I first started knocking off drug stores. A company named Geigy previously manufactured them. Now they are made by Bristol Institutes. Preluden no longer packed the punch they did in the old days but were still very powerful and effective. The old Preluden used to have a rush with which no other drug in the world could compete. A ten pill shot would send a ball of fire rushing from your gut up through your throat, causing you to exhale sharply what felt like smoke and fumes from the fire ignited within.

Desoxyn, made by Abbot Laboratories, is the cleanest and purest form of amphetamine you can obtain from a pharmacy. Desoxyn are unique little yellow pills from which it is easy to extract the dope for injection. Even when wet, they retain their shape. When soaked in water for a few hours, the water turns yellow as the methamphetamine hydrochloride is absorbed from the pill, and the pill, which becomes like a small sponge, turns white.

"Are you sure, no Desoxyn?" I asked, as we dug through the pile of boxes and bottles, searching in vain for our favorite.

"Nope, it's not here. Well, I'll get a rig, and we can blast off with Mr. Preluden," suggested Henry.

"No, let's wait. I'll call Debbie; she's expecting to go out with me tonight anyway. She has a VISA card, and we'll get her to take us to Jacksonville and rent a hotel room just in case the cops somehow suspect us and come here."

I always preferred being out of pocket after a robbery just in case the law came after me. If I was not where they expected to find me, I had a greater chance of being alerted and able to flee.

"Okay man, you call her. But it will take her a while to get here and we have plenty of time to do a shot before she arrives," proposed Henry. As he lifted his weight from the waterbed to stand, the tempermental mattress ejected five or six pill bottles onto the floor.

"No! We wait until we are out of here before we shoot any dope," I demanded, deliberately taking the forty-five out of my pants and laying it on the bed beside me before I retrieved the bottles from the floor. It was a threat, but not one I was prepared to follow through on. Had Henry bucked me and insisted on doing some dope, I would not have shot him. I would have only beaten his ass. I was getting tired of having Henry around, and was looking forward to having Debbie as a house-mate, the minute she no longer needed her parent's permission.

Henry looked at the gun then at me. I guess the warning I had given him in the car was still ringing in his ears, for he gave no further opposition to my plan. "Okay, Bill. Have it your way. You're the boss."

With the issue decided, I walked into my bedroom, which, though lacking the posters of Henry's room, still managed an impoverished ambiance. I had never really lived anywhere long enough to collect the mementos that transform a place into a home. Retrieving a hand-me-down suitcase from the closet, I returned to Henry's room and carefully laid it on the waterbed.

"Put all the dope in this and pack some clothes or towels around it so those damn bottles don't rattle so much. I'll call Debbie."

Debbie, a pretty twenty-year-old who was my current girlfriend, lived west out the Old Conway Highway. I will never forget the first time I laid eyes on her. It was at her former boyfriend's apartment, and she was wearing what we later jokingly referred to as her "Hee Haw" shirt. The shirt was dark blue, low cut and skin tight, with a fit that accented her healthy thirty-six inch breasts, thrusting them up until they threatened to spill from their tight confinement. Looking at her you would believe that if you watched long enough, and, if she made just the wrong/right move, you would be rewarded with a spectacular sight as gravity exerted more force than the modest material could bear.

I could hardly take my eyes off her that first night. The combination of her long, brown hair, beautiful body, and eyes that defied my ability to name their color, was more than enough to make me wish she were mine. Even to this day, I cannot assign one specific hue to those mysterious eyes.

Debbie and I had been together for about six weeks and had often discussed her moving in with me. Mrs. Harris, her mother, was very much against the idea and had harbored a significant dislike for me since Debbie first broached the subject.

When Debbie answered the phone, I was very cryptic. Telling her to pack a few clothes and get to my apartment as soon as possible, I told her to remember to bring her VISA card.

"What's going on?" she asked.

"I'll explain later. Just get here as fast as you can."

"Okay. I'll be there in about thirty minutes."

True to her word, exactly thirty minutes after hanging up the phone, she parked her 1978 black Z-28 beside Henry's beat up Regal. Henry and I did not even give her time to get out of the car before we strolled from the apartment with the suitcase of drugs. I opened the passenger door and leaned the bucket seat forward. After placing the suitcase in the back seat, I stood aside, allowing Henry room to maneuver his prosthetic leg into the cramped rear foot-well.

Debbie just sat there looking confused as I climbed in and told her, "Drive to Jacksonville, Baby."

"Why are we going to Jacksonville?"

"Ask me no questions, and I'll tell you no lies," I replied, quoting one of the Rolling Stones' more popular, though not original lines.

Debbie tilted her head, causing her long brown hair to cascade over one shoulder, and looked at me. She then turned towards Henry and searched his face for an explanation. Finally, after shrugging her shoulders, she backed out of the parking space and drove her perplexing passengers to Jacksonville.

I asked her to take the Air Base exit and to drive to the Ramada Inn® located on the service road east of US 67-167. "Don't park right in front of the office."

She stopped the car fifteen yards south of the office and turned to me, "What now?"

"Go inside and rent a room for three people." I had enough experience with hotels that I knew not to make the simple mistake of trying to pay less by claiming to have fewer people staying in the room than were actually present. "If someone acts suspicious, or asks, tell them your parents are visiting from out of town and are staying in our apartment," I instructed.

In just a few minutes she returned, swinging a hotel room key by its green plastic tag. Back inside the car she announced, "Room 247, around back."

We drove around the hotel and parked the car directly in front of room 247, an upstairs room. Debbie headed straight to the room, leaving me to unfold Henry from the back seat and bring the suitcase. I could tell she was wary of our baffling behavior, but I figured the contents of the suitcase would settle her down and get me back in her good graces.

As Henry followed me into the room and shut the door, Debbie, who was sitting on one of the Queen-sized beds, asked me, "Now will you tell me what in the world is the big mystery?"

By way of explanation, I put the suitcase on the bed beside her and opened it saying, "Happy New Year!"

Her mouth dropped open and those beautiful multi-colored eyes grew wide in astonishment as she saw what the suitcase contained. "Bill, what have you done?" She whispered.

Henry, who had not said a word since we entered the car, bellowed, "We robbed a drug store!"

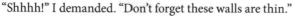

"Shhhh!" I demanded. "Don't forget these walls are thin."

Debbie was not a doper. She was raised Catholic: midnight mass, private schools, Hail Marys, the works. The most she had ever done was smoke a little pot. A single tear formed in her right eye and rolled reluctantly down her soft cheek. All she could manage to say was, "Bill?"

Forgetting my earlier admonition, I exploded, "Screw the tears! Yes I robbed a drug store!"

My anger was derived from my misjudgment of her reaction. It was inconceivable to me for her not to be ecstatic at the amount of dope we had stolen. Instead of the smiles and exhilaration I expected, she burst into tears. I read that as condemnation.

Henry wasted no time observing our domestic dispute. His focus was entirely on rummaging through the suitcase for two big spoons, a syringe, and a bottle of Preluden. Heading directly to the sink, he filled a plastic hotel cup with water. "Come on Bill. Let's get high!"

Leaving Debbie to solve her emotions on her own, I joined Henry at the table by the door and started chipping the chalk coating off the big pink Preluden 75's. I usually washed the chalk coating off, revealing the waxy white inner pill—the good part. When in a hurry, chipping the coating away expedited the process, and we were in one hell of a hurry.

Within ten minutes, the tabletop was covered with chipped chalk dust, and I had ten Preludens crushed in my spoon. I added two syringes full of water (2 cc's), pulled out my Zippo lighter, and started cooking the dope. Preluden has to be cooked to release the dope from the waxy inner pill. The longer it is cooked, the better the shot. Needless to say, I was not about to cook mine for long. I was ready to blast off now! There was plenty of time for long cooks and plenty more dope.

I poured some cold water onto a washcloth from the bathroom. The hot spoon hissed as I lowered it onto the cloth to cool the dope. Drawing boiling liquid into a plastic syringe was a sure way to get plastic poisoning, a sickness of chills and aches sufficient to induce a death-wish.

After my shot had cooled, I tore apart one of my Kool cigarettes, pulled a small piece of cotton from the filter, and dropped it into the liquid. Placing the needle on the cotton, I carefully strained the dope, making sure none of the waxy part clogged the point or entered the syringe. This process completed, I turned to Henry and asked him to hold me off.

He took hold of my left arm, squeezing tightly so the veins protruded well above the surface. Taking aim at a bulging vein, I placed the needle over an imaginary bulls-eye and pushed ...

WRIGHTSVILLE UNIT

Waking with a start, my heart racing, I sat up on my rack. Beads of sweat formed on my brow as I recalled the past experiences I had been reliving in a nightmare. "What a horrible feeling!" I thought to myself, determined to never allow another needle in my arm. My nightmare was so real! I had actually felt the point of the hypodermic needle puncture the surface of my skin.

Waking up to find myself in bed at the Wrightsville Unit of the Arkansas Department of Correction, serving a fifty-year sentence without parole, I was actually relieved. I lifted a green Kite tobacco pouch from my locker box and rolled a cigarette. The semi-dark room shook with the elaborate dream that seemed so real.

I began thinking about Debbie, wondering what had happened to her. After my arrest, she had given me the joy of becoming my wife, but I had not seen or heard from her since our divorce in 1987. And Henry … I wondered what had ever happened to ol' peg-legged Henry who had driven for me during two other drug store robberies. I had not seen him since 1982. How had the last decade treated them? For me, it had been a hell of my own design.

CHAPTER TWO

Drive Me to The Side Door

Racing and hunting madden the mind,
Precious things leads one astray.

Dawn eventually succeeded in chasing away a disturbing dream of a restless night. Yet, even with the coming of the sun, the tendrils of the night's dreams refused to release their hold on me. I could not shake the feeling that there was a purpose for the timing; the seeming reality the shadow cast over my soul.

The following day seemed to last an eternity. Now I have received a Library of Congress certification in Braille transcription. My prison work is transcribing textbooks for blind children. As fulfilling and consuming as that task is, I still have difficulty concentrating on my work. The dream caused me to question my commitment to the change I previously accepted as complete. What would call up an experience so obviously best left in the quagmire from which I have struggled so hard to extract myself? Is it a buried yearning for or a glorifying of the past I claim to abhor? The strong desire for the shot of speed I was injecting in my dream had frightened me. I was certain I would never know that desire again and even though it was a dream, there was no escaping the harrowing feeling which followed me into the light of day.

Finally, back in the barracks that afternoon, I lay on my bed and turned my thoughts to a past I had previously feared to explore. Introspection is the price I must pay to answer the questions that surfaced in the dream.

✗ ✗ ✗

"Baby, I'm going to the store. Do you need anything?"

Knowing I was lying to Debbie did not cause me one moment of concern. A dozen days had passed since the Blake robbery. The dope was gone, and I was on a path that would not end until death or the law secured me in its grasp.

"Yes, would you pick up a pack of cigarettes?" She answered without any suspicion of my devious intent. After Debbie's reaction to the last robbery, I was not about to reveal my compulsion to hit another store and refill the coffers with dope.

It was an early Saturday morning, January 12, 1980. Debbie was watching a movie on HBO in the apartment she and I now shared. Henry had moved out by mutual consent. We had not parted as enemies, though a few days together shooting speed had forced the final breach in our already cracked relationship. Continued abuse of amphetamines causes psychotic behavior. When two psychotics are in close proximity over an extended time, there is bound to be violence, and violence was the deciding factor that convinced Henry to move.

Three or four days of continuous injections of speed after the Blake robbery had fogged my memory. The details were difficult to recall. Debbie's frustration with being cooped up for days on end with Henry and me was seared into my memory. For days, I refused to relinquish the syringe long enough to even eat a meal. Debbie did not use drugs and, therefore, had an appetite. Since Henry and I would not eat, she was forced either to go out and eat alone or call for room service. Hating to dine alone, room service was her usual option. For Henry and me, the arrival of room service was a major event that required preparation. For Debbie, our paranoia was a source of utter frustration.

After announcing that she was hungry and asking if we also wished to eat— which we always declined—Debbie followed by saying, "Bill, I'm going to call room service."

"Okay, Baby. Hang on just a minute, will you? I've got to finish this shot," was my usual reply. It did not matter that I'd had twenty shots before that particular shot, and would have had twenty shots after that. *That shot* was the shot that was important. Watching the entire process from her seat on the bed, Debbie waited patiently as I continued to cook my shot, add water, cook my shot, add water, cook my shot. After each injection she would again announce, "Bill, I'm going to call room service now."

"Hang on just a minute, Baby. Let Henry finish his shot."

Again she would wait patiently as Henry cooked his shot, added water, and cooked his shot. By that time my rush had worn off, and I would begin preparing another injection.

"Bill, don't fix another shot yet. I'm going to call room service as soon as Henry is done."

"I'm not, Baby, I'm just doing this while we wait for Henry to finish."

By the time Henry had injected his Preluden, I had begun cooking my next shot. Debbie, now in a state of total frustration, would pick up the telephone and say, "I'm calling room service right now."

"Hang on a minute, damn it! Can't you see that I'm almost through with this shot?" I'd yell at her. But by the time I had finished, Henry had already begun his preparations and the cycle continued.

When she finally did get to call room service, we had to gather all the dope lying out in the open and stash it somewhere. Henry and I would then go hide in the bathroom lest some porter delivering Debbie's meal see us and wonder at our wild

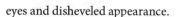

eyes and disheveled appearance.

Unable to tolerate the hotel room any longer, Debbie delivered an ultimatum: either we return to the apartment or she was going home. The poor girl did not realize that the apartment would only be marginally better than the hotel. We still refused to go eat. She was forced to go shopping for groceries by herself and to cook meals only she would eat.

I am not sure how, but she finally extracted a commitment from me to take her out. I had agreed to take her to the Checkmate Club, North Little Rock's only claim to a decent nightclub. Henry and I ate a few barbiturates to bring us down enough to face the outside world then took turns showering.

In the apartment's one main bathroom, located upstairs between the two bedrooms, Debbie was applying her makeup. Henry was in the half bath downstairs blow-drying his hair. I waited on the couch in the den for him to finish so I could do the same. Neither of us had slept since the robbery. We were hallucinating, a common result of shooting speed and not sleeping for 96 hours straight. As I waited for Henry to finish in the bathroom, I heard him speaking to someone through the partly opened door. I could not understand what he was saying over the racket of the blow dryer, so I asked loudly, "What did you say?"

There was no answer to my question and the conversation in the bathroom continued without interruption. Wondering to whom he was talking, I left my seat on the couch and approached the bathroom doorway. Careful not to let Henry catch sight of me, I peeked in the bathroom and saw him standing in front of the mirror with the blow dryer in his right hand. Gesturing with the dryer, he emphasized the dialog he was conducting with an imaginary person. Henry was in the bathroom alone, talking to someone only he could see!

I do not know why this disturbed me so much, since it was something I had been guilty of many times over the last few days. When I yanked open the door, Henry jumped . Then I exclaimed, in a disgusted voice, "Just who do you think you are talking to?"

Turning from me to his previous position, Henry searched for the person with whom he had been conversing. I could see the puzzlement on his face as he realized there was no one else present. He tried to cover his embarrassment. "Nobody! I was just talking to myself."

"No, you weren't. You were hallucinating and talking your fool head off to someone who isn't here. Stop screwing around and hurry up," I demanded, as I slammed the door.

He finally relinquished the bathroom and I started drying my hair. Then, one of my old girlfriends came in and we talked as I prepared to go out. Suddenly the bathroom door was jerked open and Henry stood in the doorway with a look of triumph on his face. In a sarcastic whine, he asked, "And who are *you* talking to?"

Rudely snapped back to reality, all my real and fabricated animosity towards Henry came rushing out, and I sprang from the bathroom. Grabbing him by the throat, I tried to strangle him. Debbie was just coming down the stairs as Henry's prosthetic leg collapsed and we landed on the couch. I was on top, and after releasing his throat, I began throwing punches at his face. He did not have a chance. With only one leg, there was no possibility of defending against the onslaught as I pounded him deeper and deeper in the couch with each blow.

At some point I realized Debbie was on my back and screaming. She attempted to limit the force of my blows by pulling against the arm with which I struck Henry, "Bill, stop it! You are going to kill him!"

I do not know how long she had been trying to stop me. It seemed as if I could hear the echo of her voice for some time before the red finally faded from my sight and my rage abated. Henry was unconscious, his face badly swollen and bruised. After that incident, Henry decided he would rather live elsewhere.

X   X   X

"Cigarettes all you want?" I asked, clearing this unpleasant incident from my mind.

A slight nod was Debbie's only reply as I walked out the door. I climbed in the Z and headed to Bobby's house on Kiehl Avenue, just a few blocks from my apartment.

Bobby, who was twenty-seven, had recently returned from Atlanta. Not having found a place of his own, he was temporarily living with his parents. Bobby was waiting when I pulled in front of his parents' house and honked the horn. He exited the house before the echo of the car's horn died in the quiet morning air and ran to the car with his two-foot long, brown hair stretched on the trailing breeze. His appearance left no doubt as to his place in society—a 70's hippie who refused to accept the fact that long hair and headbands were a thing of the past. The only concession he was willing to make to the new era was exchanging bell-bottoms for worn-out, straight-leg blue jeans.

"Doo Da?" He asked as he pulled the car door shut.

"Doo Da," I responded, backing the car up and pulling back onto Kiehl Avenue.

The term "Doo Da" comes from my early days of knocking off drug stores. It is from an old Grateful Dead song, "Truckin": "Trucking like a Doo Da Man," as the lyric goes. I am not exactly certain how it came to be applied to robbing drug stores, but it was the code word my friends and I used when we had already knocked-off a store or were going to rob one. Pete Battles, the guy who stuck the first needle in my arm, and who Bobby and I were on our way to see, was the first person I can remember having used the term.

The first time I used it was 1972, just after Little Mike and I had burglarized our first drug store. We did not have a car, so we walked to Lakehill Drug on JFK Boulevard in North Little Rock. I cut the bars from the bathroom window with a hacksaw as Mike kept watch. After gaining entry and stealing all the dope, we were forced to bury the majority of it in the nearby woods. With our pockets full of Preluden and syringes, we walked back to where we were living in a small room beneath a friend's house.

After passing the night in that little crawl space, we made our way to Ray Kingman's house. Ray, a short, stocky fellow with dark hair and glasses who looked amazingly like Radar on the television show, *M*A*S*H*,* and who of course was subsequently nicknamed "Radar", wavered between being a jock at school and one of my delinquent followers. His parents had already left for work, and Radar was preparing to go to school. After hearing our tale and seeing some of the evidence of our riches, it was not very hard to persuade him to skip school. Little Mike, Ray, and I piled into Ray's Camero and drove to where the treasure was buried. After retrieving our drugs and returning to Ray's, I called Pete. When he answered the phone, my intro was "Doo Da."

Pete Battles is the only person I have ever known who could keep up with me shooting speed. Actually, it was me who could eventually keep up with him; he had been at this for years. I was only a budding dope fiend, just entering the realm of the *Speed Trap*, while Pete was an experienced speed freak, long within its clutches. Pete was always willing to help with the work after a pharmacy robbery and was helping inventory our haul within thirty minutes. He was soon doing shots that would have killed me, and he personally reduced the amount of Desoxyn we had stolen at an alarming rate. Pete used to brag about having taken a physical at the age of twenty-one and the doctor telling him he had the insides of a forty-five year old alcoholic.

Bobby asked a question that fetched me back to the present, "Do you have a store in mind?"

Pete, Bobby, and I had discussed the possibility of hitting a store today. Last night, when I dropped Bobby off at home, I had told him I would think about it, and, if Debbie could be talked out of her car, I would pick him up this morning.

"No. We'll just go pick Pete up, drive around, and find one."

"What about one of the stores you have done before?" he asked.

"Nah, I don't think so. I thought about some of them last night and was kind of leaning towards Economy in Pike Plaza, but we're really not ready for one that big and there isn't another one in town I'd really like to do again."

Economy is one of the stores I had been busted for robbing in 1976 along with Matt Blake, a six-foot, six-inch tall, gangly giant, my long and one-time best friend. Matt, being the good friend he was, had given the law all the information needed for us to be given credit for that particular robbery. It was one of the three pharmacies that had netted me three concurrent ten-year sentences. Economy is a big store and the only one that I had someone else go inside to help me rob. I figured neither Bobby nor Pete was capable of that kind of involvement, and I knew I did not want to go it alone.

When we arrived at Pete's, Bobby and I climbed out of the Z and walked to the door. Pam, Pete's wife, answered our knock and invited us in. We sat in their den as Pam went to get her husband.

She soon returned to the room, her face awash with apprehension, and said, "Pete will be right out." Then, looking hard into my eyes, she asked, "What are you all up to this morning?"

I could tell by her tone and the looks I was receiving that she was leery of our business with her husband. Had this been an evening visit, there would not have been the slightest suspicion. Yet, because it was a Saturday morning, not the usual operating hours for dopers, and because Pam was very well aware of my past, her suspicions were aroused.

"We're going to go looking at cars. I've decided that it was time I found a good car and stop relying on Debbie's."

Before she could drill us further, Pete walked into the room and announced, "I'm ready. Let's go."

"When will you be home, Pete?" Pam asked.

"When I get home," Pete replied. .

The sound of breaking glass followed us out the door, and Pete said, "I think she's pissed."

I knew I had just made an enemy but thought I could turn her around by giving her some good dope after we hit our lick, since I had no doubt that we would score,

After driving a short distance down Pike Avenue, I turned on 15th Street and headed for the freeway. As we took the on-ramp to I-30 east, I pulled a joint from my cigarette pack and lighted it. After a deep hit off the joint, I offered some to Bobby and Pete. Both refused. I was the only one of us who still smoked pot. Most drug shooters become bored with weed and leave it for the harder stuff. I still loved it and was not the least bit put off by the fact that they would not partake. Regardless of the amount of "shooting dope" I had, or how high I was on it, I could always be counted on to have a stash of pot.

As the scent of marijuana filled the car, Pete asked, "Got any ideas which store you want to do?"

"I think we'll go look at Ray's on Kavanaugh," I answered.

"Why that one?" questioned Bobby.

"Because it has a good getaway."

"What do you mean?" continued Bobby.

"Well, that's one of my first requirements. The store must be in a location that allows me to get into the getaway car unseen. The last thing I want is somebody in the store being able to look out and see the car. Ray's has an alley in back. I think we could park at the Safeway store near there and not be seen. We'll check it out. Hell, we're in no big hurry. We've got all day."

"Right," responded Pete.

X X X

We spent the day staking out and, for various reasons, rejecting one store after another. Ray's was turned down because the getaway was not as promising as I had hoped. One pharmacy on Cantrell was rejected because I did not think it would carry enough dope to justify the risk. Still another was avoided simply because I had a bad feeling.

Our search finally brought us back to North Little Rock. As we drove down MacArthur Drive, I spotted a likely target. The strange thing about this store was that I had never noticed it during my many years in this occupation. At first glance, it looked perfect, and after closer inspection, it looked even better.

"Lyons Pharmacy, why have I never noticed you before?" I asked as we drove past for the third time.

"Do you like it?" asked Bobby. He was excited and not alone in the feeling. The atmosphere inside the car had changed. It was charged with a tangible electricity. This is the one!

"Yeah, I like it. I like how the side door opens onto the parking lot, and there aren't any windows on that side of the store. We could park right there at the door without attracting any attention and without anyone being able to see the car."

The pharmacy was part of a small shopping center that housed a donut shop, a gun store, and a small grocery store. The drug store was at the north end of the building and had parking available in front and along the side. It was the side parking lot and the side door which I really liked. An additional point in its favor was the fact that I was partial to pharmacies located in small shopping centers with bright orange Rexall signs adorning their fronts. I liked shopping centers because there were more people moving around and I was less likely to attract attention. Bright orange Rexall signs, tended to, proclaim substantial quantities of drugs.

As I turned off MacArthur Drive onto Lynn Lane, a side street which had access to the side parking lot, I continued, "We could drive right out of the parking lot onto this road without ever having to drive in front of the store."

Further exploration of this street revealed another attribute that helped me decide that this was indeed the one. About a block further down Lynn Lane was a small apartment complex called Parkway. As we drove past, I pointed out to my accomplices that this would be a perfect place to park a switch car and asked Pete, "Could we borrow your car to park there?"

"Sure, but I don't want Pam to know anything about it."

"Hell, I won't tell her. As far as I am concerned, God will not know unless you tell Him."

"Are you sure you can get that pistol?" I inquired of Bobby.

"No problem. I've already put it in my room. My parents are out of town and won't even know we used it. I almost brought it with me when you picked me up."

"It's a good thing you didn't. It isn't a good idea to have any guns on us when we're out shopping for a store. If for some reason we attract a cop's interest, a gun would be hard to explain. We could wind up with an attempted robbery charge when we haven't done anything."

"Okay, this is the plan," I continued. "Whenever I do a store, I always give my partner half regardless of his involvement. Since there are three of us on this one, we will split it in thirds. Bobby, I want you to drive. We'll use the Z for the robbery. You'll park it at the side door where I'll get out. Pete you will provide the switch car and …"

"Hey man," interrupted Pete. "You know, I don't want to be directly involved. I won't drive the switch car. As we agreed yesterday, I'll sell your dope for you at your price."

I had learned a long time ago not to be involved in selling dope. I always liked to find one person whom I deemed trustworthy enough to turn the pills for me. If the cops had no good leads after a pharmacy robbery, they turned to their snitches on the street and put out feelers for someone selling pharmaceuticals. Selling store dope put me in contact with too many people. With my reputation, it would have been like putting up billboards with my face on them that read, "It was me!"

"No problem. You just make damn sure that you take care of my dope. I'm giving you a full third just so you don't feel shorted and so you aren't tempted to screw me around."

"I got you, man. You get the dope. I'll look out for you," promised Pete.

"All right, Bobby. You'll drive me to the side door where I'll get out. I'll walk in the front door with a ski mask rolled up like a toboggan cap. After entering the store, I'll pull it over my face and rush the pharmacist. I'll have him sack the dope in a pillowcase, and I'll exit the side door. We'll drive away just like nothing has happened and go up Lynn Lane to Parkway apartments where Pete's car will be parked. You'll take the dope, the mask, and the gun and drive slowly back to your parents' house. I'll drive the Z. If the car is spotted in the robbery and the cops pull me over, there won't be any incriminating evidence in it. I'll also switch shirts. I have one in the back seat that my little brother gave me for Christmas."

"Yeah, that will work. Nobody will be able to connect me to the robbery since I wore a mask, have on a different shirt, and no dope, gun, or mask."

"We'll meet at your parents' house," I continued, "where I'll park Debbie's car. Then, we'll drive over to Pete's together. Pete, will Pam flip out when we get there with all that dope?"

"Nah. She won't care just as long as we get her good and high."

"That won't be any problem. Hell, we'll get her as high as she wants! Okay, that's the plan. Now we need to go buy a ski mask and pick up the pistol. I also want to stop and pick up a half-pint of Baccardi 151."

It was not that I required any liquid courage, just that I felt a half-pint of 151 put me in the right frame of mind to pull a robbery. It made me crazy enough, wild enough, and ruthless enough to do what had to be done in case things went wrong. I had no doubts about what I would do if forced to shoot it out. The rum allowed me to project a desperate enough image that my victims would not have any doubts either. Fortunately, I had never fired a shot in any robbery—a fact that was soon to change.

CHAPTER THREE

Apologetic Robber

Amass a store of gold and jade and no one can protect it.
Claim wealth and titles and disaster will follow.

Fanned by the fumes of the rum I had consumed, a fire burned hotly within me. I was psyched out, pumped up, and ready to rock-n-roll. Had the police been able to peer inside my head, had the prosecutor been able to prove my intent, and a jury aware of facts yet to unfold, I could already have been charged, tried, and convicted. Only one thing separated the actual fact of the robbery from my intent: I had not yet walked through the front door of Lyons Pharmacy.

On numerous occasions prior to robberies, I had been asked by my partners, "Are you sure about this?"

My standard response to this inquiry was, "They can go ahead and charge me. This thing is already done!"

With Bobby at the wheel, we drove past the Parkway Apartments where Pete's 1976 Oldsmobile 98 was parked. In the early evening darkness, I could barely discern its shape from the other cars in the parking lot, but it was there, unoccupied and waiting to deliver Bobby from the vicinity once we pulled our caper.

ROBBER APOLOGIZES FOR SHOT

A masked robber apologized to two employees when his gun fired during a robbery Saturday of a North Little Rock drugstore, according to a police report.

ARKANSAS DEMOCRAT—MONDAY
JANUARY 14, 1980   11 C

Turning my eyes from the switch car, I looked down the road as Lyons came into view. It was suppertime, and the sun had cooperated by leaving us without its revealing light. Noticing the darkness, I checked my watch. The time was just after six p.m., and everything looked and felt perfect. There was only one car in the side parking lot. Traffic on MacArthur was minimal, and I had not seen a cop for at least an hour—good signs if you are bent on robbery.

"Looks good, bro," I told Bobby as I inspected the positioning of the ski mask rolled up on my head to look like a cap. "Just pull in a parking spot near the side door and turn the car off. No matter what happens, you stay right there until I get back. It won't take me but a minute."

Bobby was scared to death but answered with as much confidence as he could instill in his voice, "I got ya, man. Good luck!"

Climbing from the car, the 22 long barrel pistol I had stuffed down the front of my blue jeans stabbed me in the top of my thigh. Wincing from the pain, I slammed the Z's door shut and started my march to the front door. This was always the hardest part. It was the time when all my doubts rocketed to the surface, and I was faced with an almost paralyzing trepidation. It was the time I confronted death, knowing these few seconds could be my final moments alive. There was still time to back down, although I never did. I was more terrified of possible ridicule from fellow robbers than from anything that might actually happen to me during the robbery. I felt I would rather die than look at myself in the mirror and have to say, "Coward!" Not once in all my years of robbery did I ever reach this point and back out. Like I said, "They can already charge me. It's done!"

With one final deep breath, I charged the double glass front doors of the pharmacy. It seemed to take superhuman strength to force my way through those glass doors. They resisted my efforts, almost as if they knew my ill intent. However, as soon as the barrier had been broken, I was again in my element. Instantaneously, I was converted from an ordinary, frightened young man of twenty-four, dressed in jeans and a red flannel shirt with a blue stocking cap, into an armed lunatic, whose wild eyes loomed through the holes of the ski mask, searching for a victim.

In one swift movement, I pulled the mask over my face with my left hand and the gun from my pants with my right. At my sudden appearance, a startled young man, whose boyish face I pegged as a high school student employed stocking shelves, turned to flee. He was nowhere nearly fast enough. With my left hand, I grabbed him by the back of his shirt collar. Being careful to keep him between the pharmacy area and me, I propelled him as fast as possible towards the back of the store. Pharmacists are well known by those in my line of work to carry or keep loaded weapons in their stores. I always made it a point to get the drop on them by either keeping them unaware of my intentions until they were looking down the barrel of my drawn gun or grabbing a hostage that could be kept between them and me. I wanted to make certain that if any pharmacist wanted to be a hero, it would not be accomplished at my expense.

Forcing the young man rapidly down an aisle towards the pharmacy area with my pistol at his back, I cried out, "Pharmacist! Pharmacist!" I could not see him, and I was almost at the back of the store. My hostage was trying to say something to me, but I was not paying any attention to him. I continued to search for the pharmacist and yelled, "Pharmacist! Pharmacist!" I was afraid that the pharmacist was in the back room and would make a sudden appearance with a shotgun loaded with 00 buckshot that had my name stenciled on each pellet.

Finally, the young man's words got through to me, "I am the pharmacist!"

I had just shoved him through the hinged, waist-high double doors, which separated the pharmacy from the rest of the store, when I grasped what he was saying. Spinning him around, I asked him, "What did you say?"

"I am the pharmacist," he answered, and I noticed that he was older than I had thought and was wearing a white pharmacist's smock.

"Well damn!" I exclaimed, as all of the tension went out of me. It was as if someone had turned off a switch within me, and I immediately calmed down. I was in control and feeling the power, which was as addicting and exhilarating as any narcotic.

From our raised position, I scanned the store. Failing to see any other employees or customers, I asked him, "Are you alone?"

"Yes."

Letting go of his shirt but keeping my gun trained on him, I pulled a large grocery bag from my back pocket. We had forgotten to get a pillowcase from either Bobby's or Pete's and had to stop by a Kroger store and obtain the bag. I handed him the bag and told him, "I want all the Schedule Two's."

Schedule Two is the classification for any drug with the potential for abuse. The law in Arkansas requires that these drugs be kept under lock and key. I imagine the law was passed to lower the possibility of these drugs being stolen. However, by forcing pharmacies to keep all the good dope in one spot, it actually helped people in my vocation. Had the drugs been scattered in various locations, I would probably have been caught in one store or another while a robbery was in progress since it would have required much more time to search for and find the type of drugs I wanted.

Moving slowly, so as not to make me nervous, the pharmacist took a set of keys from his pocket and began opening cabinets along the back wall of the pharmacy. There were six cabinets in a row, all about shoulder height. As he swung the last cabinet door open, he gestured to the dope inside and asked, "What all do you want?"

I was momentarily stunned as I stood there with my mouth wide open, staring into the opened cabinets. Never had I seen such a stock of drugs. I had never even heard of anyone finding such a score, not even in the old days when pharmacies stocked much more dope, when a drugstore robbery was unheard of and a burglary was a freak occurrence.

"Well?" He asked, spurring me into action.

I reached into the first cabinet and tapped a dozen or so Preluden bottles and said, "All of these." Within the same cabinet, I spotted several rows of Desoxyn and announced, "These too."

Stepping to the second cabinet, I spied an entire shelf of morphine and

Dilaudid. My knees almost buckled at the sight of these bottles, each of which represented five thousand dollars. "All of those," I whispered, tapping them with the pistol barrel. I spotted a four-ounce jar of pharmaceutical Cocaine in the next cabinet and said, "Give me that." There was a quart jar containing one hundred-milligram Demoral in the fourth cabinet, and I demanded, "That too!"

My sack was full. It did not matter what the fifth and sixth cabinets contained. I could not carry any more and did not even bother to examine their contents. Motioning for the pharmacist to give me the bag, I then told him, "Let's go to the side door."

He led the way through a doorway into the back room and then to the side door, which had a screen door on the inside with a locked, metal door behind it.

"Unlock the outside door, push it open just an inch, and then lay down on the floor right there," I indicated, pointing the pistol at a spot on the floor a few feet inside the doorway.

The pharmacist complied with my instructions completely. Then, as I was attempting to hook my left elbow in the screen door while carrying the fully loaded sack, I accidentally squeezed the trigger of the twenty-two automatic, firing a shot at the spot where the pharmacist lay.

My heart jumped into my throat. Now I was a murderer. Gone was the bold, daring bandit, the daredevil image I had of myself, now replaced with the knowledge that I was a killer. Now I was a real Bad Guy who would be hunted down like a rabid dog. I had been pointing the gun directly at the pharmacist as I tried to open the screen door. I was certain I had killed him. "Are you ok?" I asked the presumed corpse.

"Yes." He answered in a voice filled with the fear one experiences when they realize they are about to die.

"That was an accident, man. You've done well. You just lay on that floor for five minutes, and you'll be ok. If you poke your head out that door, the next shot will be between your eyes," I explained to him as I exited the store.

Apparently he took me at my word because I did not see him again until he testified against me in court.

I walked swiftly to the car, and Bobby leaned over to push the passenger door open for me. As I jumped inside, he said, "Damn, that was quick!" The robbery had taken less than three minutes in the real world, but in my head time during the robbery had slowed to a crawl. Every motion was in slow motion, every sound louder, all my senses worked overtime. The pharmacist's progress to gather drugs seemed sluggish. I always pushed for quicker movements, for everyone to hurry, certain in my mind that police were racing to the scene, their arrival imminent. Even replaying robberies in my mind months later, they seemed to unfold in slow motion.

As I pulled the door shut and we exited the parking lot onto Lynn Lane, Bobby said, "Man, a dude pulled up to the front of the store right after you went inside. He never got out of his truck. I bet he watched the whole thing."

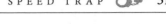

I turned around to look at the receding pharmacy and saw a red pickup truck pulling from the parking lot, coming in our direction.

"Red pickup?" I asked.

"Yeah."

"He's coming this way!" I exclaimed. We were almost at the apartments. I did not want the guy in this truck to see our switch car, so I told Bobby, "Make a block, and we'll see if he follows us. If he does, then haul ass and lose him. We'll blow off the switch car and go directly to your parents' house."

"Okay," Bobby responded, nervousness evident in his voice.

I turned to look at him, checking him out, wondering if he would fail me. He appeared to be ok, and I turned my attention back to the red pickup as we made the first turn of the block.

The truck turned the other direction, and, greatly relieved, I told Bobby, "It's ok, man. He turned the other way. Finish making the block and get back to Pete's car."

As we approached a stop sign cater-cornered from the apartments, Bobby suggested, "Why don't I just get out at the stop sign and walk across the street with the sack. That way you won't have to cross this street and can go on to my folk's house."

I took a quick survey. I pulled off the red flannel shirt and stuffed it, the ski mask, and gun into the over-full sack. "All right. That'll work," I told him.

Bobby stopped the car at the stop sign, and, as he took the sack, I picked up the license plate I had removed earlier. Leaving his door open, he climbed from the car and walked across the street. I got out and slammed the passenger door shut. Crossing behind the car, I stooped down and quickly reattached the license plate with two bolts. Once in the driver's seat and with one last glance at Bobby, who was just entering the parking lot of the apartment complex, I turned left on Parkway Drive and headed for Sherwood.

Using only the back roads, I did not see any cops on my way. "That was a piece of cake," I told myself as I pulled into Bobby's parents' driveway and killed the engine.

After a few minutes, I began checking my watch in the beam of the front porch light. Bobby should not be more than five minutes behind me. The five minutes passed … then ten. Finally, after fifteen minutes, I could not wait any longer. I knew something had gone wrong. I had to get out of the area in case the cops had arrested Bobby and he had snitched.

Shattering the quietness of the night, I started the Z, pulled back onto Kiehl Avenue, and drove to a nearby convenience store. I was scared—much more frightened than at anytime during or since the robbery—as I walked to a pay phone in front of the store. Looking up and down Kiehl, I expected to see a whole string of police cars with their blue lights flashing, speeding to my position in order to arrest me at any moment. I inserted a dime into the phone and dialed Pete's number. He answered it on the first ring, "Hello."

"Pete?"

"Yeah."

"Have you seen Bobby?" I asked.

"Yes. He's here."

"What is he doing there?" I demanded, both relieved and angry.

"You better come on over, Bill," Pete responded.

"What's wrong? What is he doing there? He was supposed to meet me at his parents."

"Just come on over, Bill," was his only reply.

I was very suspicious. I was already thinking that these guys were trying to beat me. "Is it cool?" I asked and then demanded, "He better have my stuff!"

"It's cool. Just come on over," is all I could get out of him.

"I'll be there in fifteen minutes."

After hanging up the phone, I was angrier than I ever remember being in my life. Something was rotten, and something had gone very wrong; but I had no idea what it was. All I knew was that I had hit the biggest score of my life, and if those two dopers thought for one minute I would not kill them if they tried to beat me, they were sadly mistaken.

Getting back into the car, I headed for a tale that I would never fully believe until confronted with the facts during my trial, a trial that would not find me until the fifteen thousand miles which separated us, was breached.

CHAPTER FOUR

My Dad Has a Shotgun

Love the world as your own self;
then you can truly care for all things.

WRIGHTSVILLE UNIT

"Mail call!" screamed the young officer working barracks eight, pulling me back to reality. Jumping to my feet, I went to see if any mail had come for me.

After reaching the bottom of the stack of mail, he finally found a letter for me and called out, "Bill Allen."

"Pass it back," I told the officer, standing on the fringes of the group of inmates that were gathered around him, all hoping to be as fortunate as me.

"Mail Call" is one of the few events which a inmate eagerly awaits each day. Mail Call and "Lights Out" both provide temporary escapes from the monotony of doing time. Everything comes to a halt when those letters are distributed. Domino games pause. The televisions, which are always at full volume, competing against each other for the right to be heard over the constant noise of any barracks, are turned down. Arguments are postponed. Discussions are halted. I have even seen people come, dripping wet out of the shower, with only a towel wrapped around their waist, in hopes of receiving a letter from home.

After being passed from hand to hand, the letter finally reached me. I immediately looked at the return address and was pleased to see one of the labels I had made on my computer for my nine-year-old niece, Renee.

"All right!" I exclaimed, as I showed the envelope to Dan Evans, who smiled, knowing how much the letters I received from Renee mean to me.

My nieces, with the exception of Heather who is thirteen, were all born since my incarceration. Renee is the most consistent pen pal. Kimberly, who just turned seven, writes occasionally. Samantha, my sister's daughter, writes often, but not nearly as much as Renee. Heather, who is Renee's and Kimberly's sister, and my brother's oldest daughter, sends a note now and again.

Renee and I have been playing question and answer games through the mail for almost two years. Our first game was a "History Game." I would write her, asking a question concerning history. Renee had to use her own resources to find the correct answer. The only rule is neither of us could ask for assistance from others. If she answered my question correctly, she would receive ten points. She would then ask me a question, and I must find the answer. Renee won the "History Game", fifty points to my forty, and, for her distinguished achievement, I made her a winner's certificate on my computer. Basically, computers belonging to the Department of Corrections were not to be used for personal projects. However, the computers in the Braille Project belonged to the School for the Blind. Ben Baker, the Braille Project Coordinator had approved their use for me.

We had just completed another intellectual tournament. This one was a "Science Game," which I was fortunate to win. We had been tied forty-to-forty when she failed to answer my question concerning why the calendar includes leap years. In an effort to soften the blow of her loss, I sent Renee a second-place certificate, certain that she would appreciate my humor. Second place is better than last, even if there were only the two of us playing. However, I underestimated my nine-year-old darling, as her letter soon revealed.

This one letter is all I received, so I returned to my room and again reclined on my bed. Opening the envelope, I found it contained two pages. The first was a letter written in her young script, which I had seen greatly improve over the last two years:

Dear Uncle Bill,

If you have a Bible we can play this game. Do you have a Bible? If you do, do you want to play a Bible Game? Yes or no?

If you don't, I don't mind, I have had the stomach bug. But now I feel 100% better. Have you had a good week?

On Easter, from the Easter Bunny, I got a candy breakable bunny. And from someone else I got a charm bracelet and other jewelry.

Love ya!

Renee Ann

The second page caused me to laugh aloud. "Check this out!" I told Dan as I handed it to him.

It was a certificate Renee had made for me on her computer:

SCIENCE CONTEST
AWARD
Awarded to
WILLIAM W. ALLEN
It is about time you beat this 9-year-old kid in one of our contests.
Renee Ann Allen

"Man, that is priceless!" said Dan, laughing in his rich way.

Dan is one of the two people who share this semi-private room with me at the Wrightsville Unit. Convicted of selling marijuana, he has served five years of a thirty-year sentence. Dan is one of the few people I have ever met in prison who is a joy to be around. He draws a delightful laugh, which needs no more of an excuse to spring forth than the most ordinary statement, from a seemingly inexhaustible source. Laughter is a scarce commodity in this dismal environment. I am seldom a participant in this light emotion. However, I do appreciate its sound when it is a true reflection of joy and not a forced corruption of mirth, or used to fill gaps after bad jokes.

It was Dan's laughter that first attracted me to him. When we realized we were both born on New Year's Day, he ten years my junior, the friendship was sealed. Dan is a far cry from the typical "inmate" stereotype. His neat, blond hair, blue eyes, sense of humor, and his ethics—another trait seldom present in those that share this habitat with me—make him stand out among his peers.

Dan enjoyed the moment with me, chiding me about finally winning one of the contests. I take these games very seriously. I will not allow Renee to win simply because she is a little girl. If she beats me, she truly beats me; and I hope it makes her appreciate the victory that much more.

It is very important to me that I am a good influence on my nieces. It is my desire to be a person whom they can trust—for them to know if Uncle Bill says, "X, Y, and Z" then it is, X, Y, and Z! Realizing I have a lot of ground to make up, I strive to be someone they can respect.

Laying the letter and award aside and leaving Dan to read his own mail, I turned my thoughts back to the past. Not, however, before the thought crossed my mind, "How in the world did the Bill Allen of today evolve from the Bill Allen of yesterday?"

✗ ✗ ✗

Many thoughts filled my head, and butterflies danced in my stomach as I drove to Pete's. What the hell could have happened to cause Bobby to deviate from our plan? Did Pete and he have a plan of their own? Was this a rip-off? Had Bobby been caught? Had he led the cops to Pete's? Were they now luring me there to be arrested? There seemed to be only one way to obtain the answer to my questions: go to Pete's.

"Damn!" I thought, "Why did I give the gun to Bobby?" Of course, I knew why, but that did not change the fact that I would feel a lot better approaching my uncertain destiny with a gun in my hand.

Considering and then discarding numerous possibilities, I continued my drive to Pete's. Turning off Pike Avenue, I drove past his house. Apparently, Bobby was there because Pete's Oldsmobile was in the driveway. All the lights were on in the house, but I could not see anyone through the open curtains. I continued and turned on the next street, planning to make my second block of the night. I wanted to be certain there were no cops sitting in their cars waiting to pounce upon me. I was determined that if this were an ambush, I would realize it before climbing from this fast car.

Failing to find anything suspicious, I pulled into the driveway and remained in the car, leaving the engine running and turning off the headlights. I remained seated while Pete peeked out of the back door curtain. As angry as I was, I was not certain what was going on in the house and was not in any hurry to stroll in there. Finally, Pete came outside. As he approached the car, I rolled down the window.

"Come on inside, Bill," he said.

"What's going on, Pete? You got my dope?"

"Come on in, man. Bobby is in there, scared to death. He left the dope," answered Pete.

"He what?!" I exploded. Abandoning caution, I turned off the engine, sprang from the car, and stormed into the house.

Bobby was sitting in the den with Pam, looking as if he had seen what hides under children's beds. "Where's my dope?" I demanded.

"Bill, sit down. I can explain," answered Bobby, his voice shaking at my obvious rage. I have a very bad temper and a look that will wither marble when it is evoked; I have always prided myself on my quick temper and piercing stare, both of which have gotten me into and out of much trouble. Such a temper when dealing with the unsavory characters I ran around with became a hallmark of my personality and contributed to my reputation. Knowing I was quick to anger, the people I ran around with avoided setting me off. Being feared because of that was a source of pride. The full force of these was now directed at my delinquent driver.

"Screw sitting down! Where is my dope?" I shouted, approaching him. If I had had a gun, I would have been pointing it at his head threatening to blow it off if one lie crossed his lips. The fact that Bobby was the one who possibly had a gun never crossed my mind. All I could see was the red hue of fury and a punk who thought he could beat me.

"Ok, man. This is what happened. After I got out of the car and you turned to drive away, I was walking to Pete's car, and, man, all hell broke loose! There were cops everywhere!"

Bobby paused here and attempted to rise from the couch. Taking a threatening step forward, I did not allow him to get up. Flustered and frightened by my demeanor, he continued from his sitting position.

"I could see Lyons from the apartments, and three cop cars pulled up there. One of them drove back out and started heading directly towards me. Then, another one was coming from the other direction in front of the apartments. They both had their lights and sirens going. I just knew they were coming for me, and I thought I better stash the dope. So, I stuck it underneath the outside stairwell of one of the apartments. Then, I started walking towards the car, as if I had just left an apartment, and one of the cop cars turned into the apartment parking lot. He drove through real slow and put his spotlight on me. As I reached Pete's car, he sped off."

"So, I just left the dope there and came over here," he offered.

"Well, you can just go back and get it," I told him, none of my rage abated. I did

not buy this story and was not going to let him think for one minute that I did. I knew dope fiends and realized they could not be trusted. Most of them would steal from their mothers. I did. I had no doubt that Bobby would steal from me if he felt he could get away with it. I was determined to let him know that he could not.

"Ok, I'll go get it. Are you going to come with me?"

"Hell no! I did my part. Now, go get my dope, Bobby!"

"I'll go with you," suggested Pete.

"Pete, you don't have to go. You didn't leave it there," cried his wife.

"No, but he may need some help. I better go with him."

"Bring my dope back, Pete," I told him, letting him think he was the only one I now trusted. Not that I trusted him in the least at that moment, I just wanted him to feel like I was relying on him to get my stuff. My gut told me this was something they had cooked up together, and I was allowing them to back out of it by letting them go get the dope. If I was to go to this imaginary stairwell and the dope was not there, they would have to stick to their story. This way they could go out together, discuss the fact that I did not buy the story, and decide to bring me my score. I was certain that I had let them know that I would not take this lying down.

In the thirty minutes it took for Pete and Bobby to return, many frightful possibilities passed through my suspicious mind, not the least of which was that they might return with the police. As they pulled into the driveway, I was relieved to see they did not have a trail of police cars following them. As Pete and Bobby walked to the door, I was enraged to see they did not have the sack of dope.

Pete did not give me time to question where the sack was. He started in with his explanation even before the door shut behind Bobby. "Bill, the cops got the dope. The apartment complex is full of cops. There are more cops there than at the store."

"Damn!" I exclaimed as I rushed at Bobby, grabbing him by his shirtfront and shoving him as hard as I could up against the refrigerator. "You coward! See what your cowardice has caused!"

He did not even attempt to break my hold on him as his head dropped, his eyes unable to meet mine. "I'm sorry, Bill. What else could I have done?" Bobby asked.

"You could have gotten in the car and drove to your parents' as we agreed. You made it away from there, didn't you?"

"Yes, but, if I had still been carrying the sack when the cop pulled in the parking lot, he would have gotten me."

"If you hadn't taken the time to stash the sack, you would have already been in the car, and he wouldn't have seen you," I told Bobby in a disgusted tone. With one final shove, I let go of him and walked into the den.

Sitting on the couch, I tried to think of what could possibly be done now. I was starting to believe their story; what other choice did I have? If it was true, then we were all in deep trouble. Bobby sat in a chair across the room while Pete and his wife sat on the couch with me.

"Bobby, is that gun registered to your dad?" I asked him.

"Yeah, I think so," he answered, a new fear replacing the dejected expression on his face.

"Are there any more guns in the house?" I inquired further.

"My dad has a shotgun."

"When are your parents coming home?"

"Tomorrow night."

"This is what you have to do. Go home and gather up that shotgun, a stereo, and the TV and take it all to Bluehole and throw it in. Break out a window in the house. Be sure to break it from the outside so the glass falls inside the house. Then, leave the backdoor open and go over to Mary Ann's and stay with her. Don't go home until after your parents get there. When they come home and see that the house has been broken into, they will call the cops and report all that stuff stolen. That way when the cops trace that pistol back to your father, he can tell them about it being stolen in a burglary."

This is the best I could come up with on such short notice. Keeping the cops from suspecting Bobby was the important thing. If it ever came to their questioning Bobby, he had shown me enough tonight to convince me he would break weak and squeal. If he followed my instructions and set the house to look as if it had been burglarized, threw the shotgun and other items in Bluehole, a bauxite pit filled with water, went to his girlfriend's house until his parents returned, and reported the burglary, we just might get by ... might.

"Man, don't anyone say a word about what happened tonight," I instructed them. "I have to get home. Debbie is going to kill me. I better go face the music. Pete, will you take Bobby home so he can do all this, then take him to Mary Ann's?"

"Yeah, I'll do that."

"Okay, I better get going. Remember," I cautioned them, "not a word to anyone!"

With that final warning, I left them, not certain that they were telling the truth, not certain they would follow my instructions if they were. The only thing I was certain of was, when I returned to the apartment, I was going to catch hell from Debbie. On the way home, I made one stop to pick up a pack of cigarettes for her. It was the least I could do.

X X X

Five days passed without any contact from Pete or Bobby. I was beginning to think maybe, just maybe, we had pulled it off. Debbie was just starting to talk to me again after that fateful night. I knew she did not believe a word of my story about running into Henry and going out drinking, even though she never came right out and called me a liar.

The morning of January 19, 1980, I drove her to work. She had refused to allow me use of her car since the robbery, but I had talked her into it today in order to go job hunting. After dropping her off and returning home, I decided to give Bobby a call to see how things gone on his end.

A woman answered the phone, "Hello."

"May I speak with Bobby?" I asked.

"Who is this?" was her suspicious reply.

"Bill."

"Bill who?" she demanded. Bobby's parents did not know me from Adam, and the tone of his mother's voice convinced me that I wanted to keep it that way.

"Is Bobby there?" I asked.

"No! Bobby is in jail. Bill, what is your last name?"

I hung up the phone without responding. "Well, that's it," I thought. "Caca is fixing to strike the proverbial blowing device!"

Pete worked for a construction company, and, since it was raining, I thought he might be home. Picking up the phone, I called and told him about my conversation with Bobby's mother.

"Bill, have you seen today's *Gazette*?" Pete asked.

"No. Why? What's in it? What am I looking for?" I asked as I picked the paper up from the kitchen table.

"Turn to B Section, the article, "NLR resident, 27, held in robbery," he advised. Following his instructions, I found the article:

NLR Resident, 27, Held in Robbery

Robert A Futch, 27 of 6426 Claremont Street, North Little Rock, was arrested Thursday afternoon and charged with robbing the Lyon Drug Company at 4214 MacArthur Drive, North Little Rock, January 12.

The store was robbed of about $260 worth of drugs by a man with a gun, who fled in a car in which there was at least one other person, officers said. The drugs and gun were later recovered at a nearby apartment building after a man dropped the articles on the ground and fled when a police car approached. Other suspects are being sought.

"Did you guys do what I told you the other night?" I asked him after I had finished reading this disastrous article.

"No, Bobby wouldn't do it," Pete confessed.

"Damn it!" I shouted into the phone.

"Bill, I tried to talk him into it, but he just wouldn't do it."

"Well, we're busted," I told him.

"Nah man, Bobby won't tell on us," Pete tried to reassure me.

"Bull, we're busted," I repeated. "Let me know if you hear anything."

"I will. You do the same," he returned.

"Sure," I answered, hanging up the phone.

What the hell was I going to do? I did not have a dime to my name. I could not just stick around and wait for the law to come and get me. What to do? The only bright side to this was I now knew that my partner's story was not a total lie; the cops did get at least some of the drugs. I could not even muster any anger at the way the story said that the drugs were recovered, *"after a man dropped the articles on the ground and fled when a police car approached."* It did not mention anything about finding them under a stairwell.

Contemplating my options, I realized I should leave town now. However, considering how I had been wrong to suspect Bobby of ripping me off, maybe I was wrong about him snitching on me, too. Procrastinating about having to make a decision, I elected to go to Lakewood and see a friend of mine, Steve Stillwell. Steve had some crank, and we spent the day shooting dope. At four o'clock, I had to go pickup Debbie, so I left Steve without ever telling him what was happening.

Debbie was waiting for me as I pulled into the parking lot of the office where she was a secretary. As she climbed into the car, she gave me a kiss and looked at me questioning and asked, "What's wrong, Bill?"

"You remember the other day when I was gone for so long?" I asked her.

"Of course."

"Well, I lied to you. Bobby, Pete, and I robbed a store..." I confessed the entire story. She sat calmly listening to me tell her how her whole world was about to crumble.

That Debbie loved me, I did not doubt. How she would respond to my information, I could not guess.

"So," I continued, "chances are the cops are going to be looking for me. If they do, then I have to split. What I need to know is: do you want to go or stay?"

We drove for several minutes without her answering. Stealing quick glances at her, I saw her eyes fill with tears and watched the drops roll down her face, leaving dark trails of ruined mascara. Finally, as we neared our apartment, she answered me, "I want to stay."

Man, how that answer hurt! But it was what I expected. How could I expect this innocent, sweet girl to take off with me? Regardless, it hurt like hell!

"Okay," is all I could manage, emotion choking my throat.

That night was quite intense. We did not do much talking. Debbie fixed herself some supper; I was still too hyped on Steve's crank to eat. Our lovemaking was as spectacular as it was quiet. It was as if neither of us wanted to break the spell of what could very well be our last night together. Debbie fell asleep in my arms that night, and I held her close all night, unable to truly grasp what had passed between us.

I guess I did finally manage to fall asleep because morning found me in bed alone. I quickly rose and, going downstairs, found her drinking a cup of coffee at the kitchen table.

"Are you going to drive me to work today?" she asked.

"Do you want me to?"

"If you want to use the car today, I guess you'll have to," she responded.

"Ok, I'll be ready in a few minutes."

"Hurry up. I don't want to be late," answered the ever responsible Debbie.

I drove her to work and returned home. It was a beautiful day, too beautiful to be feeling this way. I was certain that I was going to have to flee, and I had no problem with that. Hell, I had hitchhiked across the country six times when I was younger. I knew I could return to the highway with my thumb out and get wherever I wanted. It was leaving Debbie that caused my turmoil. Going upstairs, I packed some of my clothes in the same suitcase into which Henry and I had put the dope from Blake. If I heard the cops were looking for me, I wanted to be prepared to make a fast escape.

As I snapped the suitcase shut, the phone rang. My stomach immediately filled with butterflies. Call it ESP, premonition, call it whatever you want, but I knew before I ever picked up that phone, it was bad news.

"Hello."

"Bill, this is Pam. The cops just came by here looking for Pete. I told them he wasn't home. They want him to come to the North Little Rock Police Department when he comes in."

I could tell she had been crying as she continued, "They said they just want to talk to him. And Bill, they were asking about you. I told them I didn't know you."

"Okay Pam, thanks a lot," I told her, hanging up the phone. Knowing I was not one of her favorite people, that she would take the time to give me this warning, surprised me. Picking up the packed suitcase, I took one last look around the apartment before closing the door on this chapter of my life.

I drove to Debbie's workplace and parked the car. Walking inside the office building, I asked a lady where I could find Debbie Harris. As I walked into Debbie's office, she took one look at me and knew it had happened, that the cops were after me. She immediately slumped in her chair, then—just as quickly—mustered her resolve, ready to face the unknown.

"Come on, Debbie. Tell your boss an emergency has come up, and you have to leave for the day."

"Okay, wait for me outside," was all she said.

She came out a few minutes later and after getting into the car, said, "I told him my sister was in a car accident."

I just nodded my head and asked her, "Do you have any money in the bank?"

"Only about a hundred dollars."

"Can I have it?" I asked.

"Sure."

"We'll go get it, and you need to drive me out the interstate as far as you can. The cops were over at Pete's and asking about me. I've got to go."

"Well, I'm going with you!" she exclaimed.

Surprised, I turned to look at her and asked, "What do you mean? I asked you yesterday if you wanted to go or stay. You said you wanted to stay."

"Yes, I want to stay with you!" she answered me, tears coursing down her cheeks.

I could not believe what I was hearing! Could this really be? Did this sweet creature really plan to abandon her family and friends, a known way of life, for me and the uncertainty of a fugitive's existence?

"Are you sure, Honey?"

"Yes," was her single response.

CHAPTER FIVE

Not Being in Any Position to Refuse His Generosity

Who does not trust enough will not be trusted.

Debbie convinced me her need for a few clothes outweighed the risk of her returning to our apartment. She deposited me at Steve's, where I would await her return as she made a quick dash home.

"Man, that's crazy! You shouldn't have let her go," proclaimed Steve, after I had briefed him on the situation.

"Have you ever tried to convince a woman that clothes are unnecessary?" I asked my friend.

Regardless of my glib answer, I was extremely nervous and worried as I constantly watched the clock hanging on the wall in Steve's den. Calculating five minutes for the trip to Sherwood, five minutes at the apartment, and an additional five minutes for her return, I became distraught when the actual time exceeded my calculations.

"I shouldn't have let her go!" I exclaimed after twenty minutes had expired. "I should have forced her to leave without clothes. Clothes, we could always get. Her, I cannot replace!"

As a small consolation, I had at least had the foresight to remove my suitcase from the car before Debbie had departed. Picking it up, Steve said, "Come on, I'll give you a ride as far as Conway."

Several times in the past, Steve had given me rides out of town as I prepared to embark on one of my many cross-country hitchhiking trips. On one of my shorter trips to New Orleans, he had even given me a ride as far east as Memphis. That he now offered a ride west, without me stating my direction of travel, was not unusual. All of my trips, with the exception of the one to New Orleans, had been westward.

"Let's give her another few minutes," I stalled, walking to the window in the living room. I was not quite ready to accept the fact that Debbie was lost to me, that I had unwittingly delivered her into the hands of the law.

Hearing a car outside, I pulled the curtains aside and was greatly relieved to see Debbie pulling into the driveway. "All right!" I shouted, turning to Steve. He still had my suitcase and extended it to me.

"Good luck to you, Bill," offered my friend.

"Thanks for everything, brother," I returned, heading for the door.

As I reached the door, Steve said, "Hang on a second." He then hurried into his bedroom while I opened the door and signaled to Debbie I would be right there.

"I know it isn't much, but maybe it will help you get a few additional miles down the road," proposed Steve, extending his hand which held a twenty-dollar bill.

Not being in any position to refuse his generosity, I accepted the offering. Thanking him once again, I left him standing in the doorway as Debbie and I drove off.

"What took you so long?" I asked Debbie as I turned to look at what she had gathered from home. Thrown haphazardly across the back seat were several articles of clothing. Sitting majestically on top of this pile was a stuffed teddy bear, complete with a torn arm and missing eye.

"I forgot Smokey and had to go back for him," explained Debbie.

Quite naturally, Smokey was the bear's name. Her answer was all the explanation or justification needed to explain her delay. Had I given the matter any thought before, I would have suspected then, as I did now, that the real reason Debbie insisted on returning to the apartment was to retrieve Smokey, her companion since she was a child.

"And Bill," continued my girlfriend, "as I was coming back down 67-167, I saw a line of four North Little Rock police cars, all of them with their lights flashing. They took the Sherwood exit, and I bet they were going to our apartment."

I had no doubt that she was correct in her assessment and cautioned her to drive carefully. We had one more stop to make before we could "get out of Dodge", the bank, in order for Debbie to close out her account. We accomplished our task and affected our escape from Little Rock on Interstate-40 West.

The day looked promising. The sky was clear of even the slightest cloud, and, although winter, the temperature was hovering around the fifty-degree mark. As we sped west, the tension in the car dwindled with ever mile we put between us and the police who sought my arrest. Passing the Morgan exit, just a few hundred yards from Debbie's mother's house, Debbie took a deep breath. Then, as she exhaled and settled down in her seat, I knew she had just come to terms with her decision to abandon her family and friends for a dubious future with a fugitive.

Leaning over the console, I gave her a quick kiss on the cheek and said, "I'm glad you're here, Baby. It tore me up to think about having to leave without you."

In response, she reached for my hand, holding it in her soft grip and asked, "Where to?"

"I'm not sure. How much money do you have?" I asked while pulling my wallet from my back pocket and extracting the few dollars it contained.

"Look in my purse. I'm not really sure what I have besides the one-hundred and fifteen dollars I just withdrew from the bank."

Taking up her purse and gathering all her money, I piled our fortune in my lap and started counting. Debbie kept glancing at me as I counted, looking hopeful that the small amount of bills would yield a greater sum than it appeared.

"One-hundred fifty-six dollars and thirty-eight cents," I announced after pulling the change from my pocket.

I was momentarily overwhelmed by the responsibility I had assumed. Although we had achieved our initial objective by eluding pursuit in Little Rock, we faced a very ambivalent future—a future made more clouded and tenuous due to our lack of funds. Had I been forced to flee by myself, with only my fate hanging in the balance, I would not have been confronted with the inadequacy I was now feeling. Hitchhiking, wholly dependent, responsible for only myself, afforded a freedom that my current situation now denied me. Were I now hitching rides with one hundred and fifty-six dollars in my pocket, I would have felt equal to any challenge. Fields beside the road would have been my bed on clear nights; overpasses would have offered shelter from storms. I would have found a cold can of beans palatable, and the miles would have been gained at others' expense.

Having Debbie dependent on me, relying on me to solve questions of survival, forbade these minimal standards of existence. Granted, having the girl I loved at my side and a nice car in which to travel were blessings, but they were the kind of blessings that led to enhanced responsibility. Debbie had never known any hunger other than that between regularly scheduled meals. She had never slept without a pillow, nor used the bathroom behind a bush; and the car required gas, which would be the biggest drain on our funds.

"Let's go to Fayetteville and see Stan Gill," I suggested. This was nothing more than a temporary solution to the quandary before us. Fayetteville is a three-hour drive from Little Rock, and this, at least, would give me some time to form a plan.

"We need to stop for gas," announced Debbie.

Approaching the first of three exits for Conway, I told her to take the last exit. We filled the tank, and I relinquished eighteen dollars, which we could barely afford, to the attendant at the self-service gas station.

It was a quiet trip north on Highway 71 to Fayetteville, both of us lost in our own thoughts. Debbie drove the entire way. I was not getting behind the wheel while we were still in Arkansas. Once at Stan Gill's apartment, we did not find a hearty reception or much help. I was a cast off from Stan's past, someone who had outlived his usefulness in Stan's life. We remained friends, but Stan had moved on with his life and was attending the University of Arkansas in search of a degree. His association with me had now become something that could come between him and a promising future.

Earlier, when I was fifteen and attending Lakewood Junior High School in North Little Rock, my parents got the first inkling that I might be using drugs.

They did not know that Stan and I were hitchhiking to Mac Arthur Park in Little Rock after school to purchase LSD. Hippy dealers used the park's legitimate traffic to mask their drug selling operation. One evening, Stan found some barbiturates in his home medicine cabinet and called me to see if I wanted to go to the park with him the next afternoon to "sell some stuff." Unfortunately for Stan and me, his father was listening in on a phone extension. His father then called my dad. The inquisition began. After our fathers talked by phone, Stan and his dad came to our house. Stan and I lied through our teeth, although we fooled none of the parents. Since there was no proof of our drug purchases, we got off with a scolding about the planned sale. Stan and I continued our friendship for several years. He helped deplete by stash of drugs from several of my early pharmacy burglaries.

Now, Stan seemed pleased to see me. He gave us twenty dollars for gas, a quarter ounce of pot and was even more pleased to see me leave. He never said anything to indicate this attitude; it was just a feeling I had that he did not want the complications a fugitive Bill Allen could bring into his life, understandably.

Darkness had descended by the time we said our farewells and resumed our journey. Tulsa was our next stop on a trek, which would carry us across the length of America three times and put fourteen thousand miles on Debbie's Camero. Tulsa fit the bill for our immediate requirements. It was out of Arkansas, just a short distance from Fayetteville, and would allow us some time to relax, hopefully enough for me to form a course of action.

We surrendered more of our cash for a cheap motel room in Tulsa, and that night I brought up the subject I had avoided all day. As Debbie had been driving, I had noticed the diamond engagement ring that her former boyfriend, Danny, had given her. Since Danny had refused to accept its return, she now wore the ring on her right hand. I suggested that we sell it. After a weak protest, Debbie agreed. Seeing her wear his ring bothered me, but we agreed for financial reasons that it should not be left behind.

The following morning we found a jewelry store that paid cash for the ring and almost doubled our fortune. Greatly relieved with the additional funds, I now thought we could actually get somewhere. My proposal of San Diego brought a light into Debbie's eyes and agreement from her lips.

Our journey began in earnest. Heading west on I-44 to Oklahoma City, we connected to Interstate-40, which runs from coast to coast. In Amarillo, it began snowing, and we decided on a more southerly route. Darkness found us traveling on Highway 27 South. As the hours clicked away, we both grew weary and discussed where we could get some rest. A steady stream of hotels flowed pass us offering temptations which we could not afford.

I noticed Debbie silently reading the signs of the motels as I drove. Passing one sign, she read aloud, "We accept Bank Americard. Bill, isn't Bank Americard now VISA?"

My jaw dropped open as it suddenly hit me. Debbie has a VISA card! I remembered her renting the room at the Ramada Inn in Jacksonville after Henry and I robbed Blake Pharmacy. "Oh, my God! I forgot all about your VISA card. Hell, we can use it for hotels, gas, and food. We can live on it. All we have to do is keep moving so they can't track us down as the receipts come in. You're wonderful!" I exclaimed as I pulled Debbie over to me and gave her a kiss on her tender lips. My praise put a smile on her face, which lit the car with its glow.

"So, pick us out a hotel, Baby," I told her.

All concerns were now behind us just as long as we kept moving and did not let the law catch up. And keep moving we did ... west on I-20, I-10, and finally Interstate-8 into San Diego two days later. Thanks to VISA and the Bank of America, we traveled in style, soon exceeding Debbie's five hundred-dollar limit, but this did not cause any problems. Gas stations, restaurants, hotels, and even liquor stores seldom checked the books for bad or overextended credit cards.

The entire trip I drilled the contingency plan into Debbie, "When they do finally catch us, don't talk to the police. Don't tell them anything but your name. I don't care if they just want to talk about the weather, don't talk to them. They do not have any evidence on me except for what Bobby, and possibly Pete, tells them, and that is not enough to convict me. They will try to get you to tell on me by scaring you. They'll tell you they will charge you as an accomplice and send you to prison. But they can't do a damn thing to you if you just don't talk to them."

I had no doubt they would catch up to us eventually. We could run and run, trying, and possibly succeeding, in staying ahead of them, but a routine traffic stop could be our undoing. Also, we would have to stop somewhere. Travel was fine, but to every journey, there is an end. The VISA card would eventually become too risky to use, and robbery as a means of support was not a consideration. As things now stood, I felt I could overcome the charge against me. If, in my flight across the country, I started committing robberies, I could very well end up with more charges—ones I could not beat.

A few days of enjoying the beaches and the warm sunshine in San Diego was all the time we could afford there. Considering different options, I consulted Debbie by asking, "Have you ever been to Miami?"

She laughed at what I was proposing and asked, "Do you want to go to Miami?"

"Sure, why not? That is the last thing they would expect."

"Well, I've never been there. Let's go," Debbie consented.

Minutes after our arrival in Miami, I was disgusted with the place. It seemed as if the entire population consisted of people over sixty-five. A quick tour of the city convinced me that Miami was not for us, and we headed north to Ft. Lauderdale. Once there, we rented a hotel room and, without going into the room, went to grab a bite to eat. Upon our return from a seafood restaurant, we found entry to our room barred by a lock on the door. It was immediately apparent that the credit card was now in the books. Its use would have to be curtailed drastically. Also obvious was the fact that we had better get out of town. There was no doubt the law had been alerted and would soon be searching for us. So we said our goodbyes to Florida, the Sunshine State.

We headed north into Georgia and stopped in Fokston, a small town just across the Florida border. There, we rented a room at a less than luxurious hotel. I felt there would be little chance the proprietor would check on our credit at this place because it was so cheap and did not appear to have much business. After signing in, we went to get something to eat at a restaurant separate from the hotel. However, more than any need for food, our trip to the diner was prompted by the desire to be away from the motel long enough to determine if the card had been checked.

Returning from our meal, we laid our anxiety to rest when we failed to find anything unusual with the room. Everything seemed to catch up with Debbie at this hotel in Georgia. To this point, our trip had been one long adventure with few concerns other than the need to keep moving. We had had a good time with our unlimited funds and carefree travel. The lock on the hotel room door in Ft. Lauderdale had brought the fantasy to an abrupt halt. Our options were now greatly reduced, and the seriousness of our situation now hit Debbie extremely hard.

Returning from the bathroom, I found her sprawled across the bed, tears streaking her face,

"What's wrong, Honey?" I asked as I sat near her, running my fingers lightly across her back.

"I miss Jenny."

Jenny is Debbie's younger sister, with whom she maintained a best-friend kind of relationship. Her tears touched my heart and influenced me to reach a decision that was more compassionate than smart. "Would you like to call her?"

"Bill, I can't do that. You said the police could have my mom's and Jenny's phones tapped. Couldn't they trace the call and come and arrest us?"

"Well, they could if we just sat around waiting on them. We could wait until morning and call just before we leave," I suggested.

"Oh Bill, could I really call her?" Debbie asked as she sat up on the bed and wiped the tears from her eyes with the back of her hand. Her entire demeanor changed in the time it took her to switch from a prone to a vertical position.

"Yeah, Baby, you can call her."

Debbie threw her arms around me and cried out, "Thank you so much, Bill. I won't talk to her long. I just want to let her know that I am okay and that I love her."

Debbie woke me early the next morning during her preparations to depart, purposely making more noise than necessary. Her task accomplished, she asked me innocently, "I'm sorry. Did I wake you up?"

I pulled my arm from beneath the covers, looked at my watch, and exclaimed, "My gosh, Debbie, it is only six fifteen."

So saying, I rolled over and pulled the covers over my head, pretending to go back to sleep. No sooner had the covers settled than Debbie pounced upon my back, saying, "Nooooo, Bill, get up!" She started pulling at the covers trying to dig me out of my comfortable position.

Having lured her within reach, I immediately spun beneath the covers, grabbed her, and threw her off me. In one swift motion, I was astride her and had her pinned to the mattress. Reaching under her arms, I started tickling her, emphasizing my words with renewed vigor in the attack, "Wake me up at six o'clock, will you? I'll teach you, little girl!"

"Stop! Oh no, Bill, I can't stand it! Please, don't, please! Not fair!" She cried out between her laughter.

Tickling is an attack I utilize often and one Debbie particularly hated since she is extremely ticklish and I am not at all. She always accused me, as she did now, of not being fair, and I always responded, "Love and war, Baby. All is fair in love and war."

After sufficiently affecting my revenge, I climbed from the bed and joined Debbie in preparing for our departure. When we had carted our few possessions to the car and had nothing left to do but walk out the door, I told Debbie she could call her sister.

"Listen, Honey," I cautioned her. "Don't stay on the phone long, and remember that the police could very well hear anything you say. Do not tell her where you are."

"I won't, Bill. I just want to let her know that I love her."

Debbie was successful in reaching Jenny and obeyed my instructions to the letter. As she hung up the phone, the tears flowed freely, and I took her in my arms, offering what comfort I could. After allowing her to cry for a minute, I announced that I wanted to call Paul Chancey to see what he had heard.

Paul is another friend with whom I had done time at the Benton Work Release Center in 1977 and 1978. However, Paul and I go back further than that. We were partners in several armed robberies and burglaries of pharmacies before going to prison. In fact, it was Paul's girlfriend who had driven for my first armed robbery in 1976. I figured if there were any news, Paul—whom I had met at a drug house on Frank Street in North Little Rock in the early 1970's—would know it.

"Hello," answered Paul's father.

"Mr. Chancey, this is Bill Allen. Is Paul there?"

I liked Paul's father and was not concerned about letting him know who I was. He was a cool, old man.

"No, Bill. He's already left," he answered.

"Okay. Thanks a lot."

"Wait a minute, son. I need to tell you something."

"What's that?" I asked.

"Bill, the FBI have talked to Paul about you. I suggest you be very careful in calling here because, if they are looking for you and know you and Paul are friends, this phone is probably tapped."

"Okay, Mr. Chancey. Thanks a lot," I responded. Immediately hanging up the phone and taking Debbie by the hand, we walked from the room.

This changed everything. I do not know why I had not considered that the FBI would get involved. Apparently, I was not thinking. Interstate flight to avoid prosecution was most definitely a federal crime and under the jurisdiction of the Federal Bureau of Investigation. The stakes in this game had just gone up.

CHAPTER SIX

See the Golden Gate

Give up ingenuity, renounce profit,
And bandits and thieves will disappear.

Knowing that the Feds were now in on the search cast a cloud over our travel that no amount of distance could disperse. We drove to New Orleans in search of a school friend of mine. Dave Gilmore had moved to New Orleans about five years ago, since then I had visited him twice, once via Greyhound. The second time I had hitched down to see Dave and his mom, Ellie.

It was Ellie who answered my knock after Debbie and I had finally found Napoleon Boulevard and located Dave's house. Ellie gave me the disappointing news that Dave was now living in San Francisco, attending a university there. Back in the days that Dave and I used to be friends in junior high, I knew absolutely nothing about effeminate males and could not pick out a gay person at a dress sale in a San Francisco flea market. It just never occurred to me that my quiet and slim friend could be gay. Even with Ellie informing me that Dave was in San Francisco, I was not suspicious. Nonetheless, it would not have affected our decision to visit him because as disappointed as we were not to find Dave in New Orleans, it gave us a destination. We were back on the road to California!

We had no more difficulties with the credit card. We made a concerted effort to be more careful with our uses of the card. Only two things of consequence happened on the trip to the "City on the Bay." One took place in Corpus Christi, Texas. We had a flat tire crossing a long bridge as we approached Padre Island. Fearful of attempting to purchase a tire for a replacement, we put the space-saver spare on the car, a tire with a recommended range of fifty miles. Amazingly, this tire carried us all the way to San Francisco and then some.

The second event occurred when we stopped for something to eat in a roadside restaurant in California. As we were eating our meal, an expense for which there was no cash to cover, we noticed the lady working the cash register was looking up credit cards in a book. There was no way the VISA could be used. Debbie and I finished our meal, enjoying it but a little, knowing we were going to have to slip out without paying.

"Ok, this is what we'll do," I told Debbie. "You take the car keys and go to the bathroom. Hang around in there for two minutes and then walk out the front door. I'll wait here like I am going to pay the bill. When you are safely out, I'll get up and follow you. You go out and start the car and wait for me. I'll drive."

"All right, Bill," Debbie answered as she stood up, picked up her purse, and walked to the restroom located between the cash register and the front door. Luckily, we had parked in the back, and there was a chance that we could make a fast escape without the car being seen if I was confronted while attempting to leave the room.

Throwing some change on the table as a tip for our waitress, I walked toward the front door. The lady at the cash register was busy ringing up another couple's charge as I passed her. Reaching the door, my thought of, "This is a breeze," was shattered as I heard a voice calling, "Sir. Sir!" I looked over my shoulder while pushing the door open and saw the lady at the cash register was still occupied with the couple. Once more, "Sir" was cried out, and I turned to look towards our table. I saw our waitress motioning to me.

"Sir, you forgot your map," she said, waving our United States Atlas in the air.

With my heart beating fast and hard, threatening to bust, I walked back to the waitress and retrieved the atlas. Thanking her, I emptied my pockets of the little change I had onto the table as an increased tip for our helpful waitress.

"Thank you," I told her.

"Thank you, sir. Have a nice day."

I walked out the front door without further incident.

"I want to see the Golden Gate Bridge before we go to Dave's," said Debbie as we entered San Francisco.

"Look at the map and see if you can tell me how to get there," I answered. I was not worried about the extra driving; we had just been across the country three times. I was not worried about the space-saver tire; it had already carried us over two thousand miles. If the lady wanted to see the Golden Gate Bridge, the lady was going to see the Golden Gate Bridge!

By now, Debbie was pretty good at giving directions from a map, and we found our way to the bridge easily. However, I did not have the opportunity to enjoy the beautiful view. As we started across the bridge, I noticed cars going the other direction were lined up at tollbooths as they came off the bridge. We did not have any cash, not even enough to pay a small toll.

"Honey, do you see anything telling how much the toll is?" I asked Debbie.

She turned around and started reading the signs for the traffic going the other direction. "Seventy-five cents," she answered.

"Do we have seventy-five cents? I know I don't have it. I gave my last bit of change to that waitress in that restaurant."

Debbie pulled out her purse and counted her change. "I've got fifteen cents."

"I don't know what we are going to do when we get to the other side."

Approaching the end of the bridge, we were greatly relieved to find that there was no tollbooth.

"I guess you only have to pay going into San Francisco," mused Debbie.

"Well, so much for turning around and going back the same way we came. See if you can figure out how to get back into town without going back across the Golden Gate Bridge."

Debbie retrieved the map from its customary place between the console and the passenger seat. After a minute of studying it, she suggested, "We just passed Sausalito; keep on 101 to San Rafael and then head east to Richmond. Once in Richmond, we can go south a little ways and at Oakland, turn west again to San Francisco."

She stuffed the map back down beside the seat and with a satisfied expression on her face, said, "No problem."

Debbie was correct with her imprecise directions, which I had no difficulty following. Her route was definitely a way back to San Francisco. However, another problem arose. Approaching the Bay Bridge, which crosses the bay between Oakland and San Francisco, there were signs advising us that a seventy-five cent toll was required at the other end.

I took the first exit that offered an escape from our present course. "Damn it! Now what are we going to do?" I exploded.

I pulled into a gas station and studied the map for a while. Our only options were to attempt one of the tolls or travel a long distance out of our way and approach the peninsula from the south, the same way we initially came into San Francisco.

"The hell with it, we'll just go back across the Golden Gate and tell them we have no money on us," I decided.

Retracing our route, we crossed the Golden Gate Bridge for the second time that day. Debbie was now driving, since there might be some sort of confrontation at the tollbooth.

When we pulled up to the booth, Debbie rolled down her window and told the lady, "We don't have any cash on us at all. Do you take VISA?"

The fat toll lady laughed and answered, "No, but you can write a check."

Debbie looked at me questioningly, and I nodded. "Ok," she answered.

Pointing to a parking area off to the side, the lady directed us, "Pull over there and go down the steps. You will find a window where you can write a check."

"Thank you," answered Debbie, rolling up her window and pulling into the area as directed.

"Bill, won't this cause us problems, writing a check on my account?"

"It's not closed, is it?" I returned.

"No, I have a dollar forty-five in it. I mean won't the police be able to trace it?"

"Yes, but what the hell, they can trace the VISA, too. Don't worry about it. Someday we can tell our grandkids how we had to write a bad check to cross the

Golden Gate Bridge."

After writing the check, we re-entered San Francisco and called Dave. He gave us directions to his apartment, which we found after some difficulty.

As I introduced Debbie to Dave, I told her, "Dave is my only Jewish friend. As a matter of fact, he is the only Jew that I know."

"Bill, I'm not Jewish. I was kidding years ago when I told you that."

I was slowly becoming aware how little I knew about my effeminate friend. It became apparent that we certainly overstayed our welcome in San Francisco. Exactly how the law caught us is still unclear to me even now. It could have been from any one of many mistakes we made in our brief, fugitive escapade. It could have been the check at the Golden Gate Bridge, our couple of uses of the VISA card in the Bay Area, the vanity license plates Debbie had on the Z, or maybe Dave got tired of his guests. However it came to be, it happened quickly.

Debbie was working under an assumed name for a temp agency as a secretary. I was working with Dave at a wine import company, being paid in cash. Since our space-saver tire had finally given up the ghost, Debbie had been riding a bus to work, and I had been riding with Dave in his van. Exactly two months after we had left Arkansas, after fourteen thousand miles of travel, and running up fifteen thousand dollars of charges on the VISA card, our vacation soon came to its end.

Dave and I pulled in front of his apartment, looking for a place to park the van. The Z was parked there, and Debbie, not having a key to the apartment, was waiting in the car for Dave and me to get home. I should have been suspicious of the two parking places, one in front of the Z, one behind it. Neither space was big enough for the van to fit. But still, two parking places in San Francisco, that close together, was strange.

Dave stopped the van, and I climbed out as he went to find a spot big enough to park. As I approached the Z, Debbie got out of the driver's seat, shut the door, and walked around the front of the car. I had opened the passenger door and was pulling the bucket seat forward, getting some shoes out of the backseat. Suddenly, I heard the squeal of tires as brakes locked up. I clearly remember hearing two sets of squeals: one in front of the Z, one behind it. I immediately pulled back out of the car and looked at the nondescript sedan that had pulled in behind our car. An identical one had pulled in front. Both cars were angled in, thus the reason for the two unused parking spots in front and behind our car, blocking the Z. Four doors opened from these two cars, four men jumped down behind the opened doors, and four guns pointed at my heart.

The driver of the car behind us was screaming, "Don't move!"

Debbie, frightened, looked at me and cried, "Bill!"

I turned slightly towards her at her cry, and the driver who was still screaming at me pulled back the hammer of a very big pistol and screamed, "I said, don't move!"

Still disobeying his instruction, I turned and looked around, looking for a place to run. All hopes of escape evaporated as I saw a man toting an automatic weapon hanging from a shoulder strap coming up from an underground stairwell behind me and another rounding a nearby corner with a pistol-gripped, pump shotgun.

"Put your hands on top of the car!" ordered the screaming driver of the rear sedan.

As I complied, he came from his safe position behind the car door and cautiously approached me. None of his friends moved. Walking up behind me, he took first my right hand off the top of the car and pulled it around behind me. As he put handcuffs on that arm, he said, "Happens quick, don't it, Billy? You are Billy, aren't you?"

"Yes, I'm Bill," I responded.

"Well," he continued. "We're just like on TV on Sunday nights; we are the FBI." For lack of a better response, I uttered one word, "Cute."

They proceeded to cuff Debbie while I protested, "She hasn't done anything; leave her alone!"

"Sorry, Bill. We have a warrant on Debbie for hindering apprehension and one on you for interstate flight," the agent advised me as he put us in the back seat of separate cars, where we were read our rights.

Knowing Debbie's mother would get her out of jail once we were extradited to Arkansas, I waived extradition. In ten days, two Pulaski County deputies came to San Francisco and flew us back to Arkansas. All the time I had drilled Debbie about this moment while we were on the run paid off while she was in jail. Unlike my two accomplices, Debbie refused to talk to the police. Questioned first by the FBI, then San Francisco City and County Police. and finally the North Little Rock Police, Debbie stayed mute. Bond was quickly arranged for her in Arkansas, and she was released.

My case was not so simple. The Feds dropped the interstate flight to avoid prosecution. It is basically a tool used by states in order to bring the FBI in on a case so that their resources can be utilized in apprehending fugitives. However, I still faced parole violations for being out of the state of Arkansas, failing to report to my parole officer. and not being employed. Additionally, I would be tried for the aggravated robbery of Lyons Drug Store. Bond on the aggravated robbery was set at fifty thousand dollars. It was a moot point, however, since a parole hold was placed on me and bond was impossible. Not that I had fifty thousand dollars, or the thirty-two hundred it would cost to pay a bondsman's fee anyway. I was to remain in the Pulaski County Jail until I went to trial for the robbery; that is, unless my parole was violated, in which case, I would await trial in prison.

The first thing I had to do was hire an attorney. Debbie's mother had already hired one for her. Fortunately, the jail provided telephone for prisoners to use and I could still communicate with Debbie. I had one idea how this could be accomplished with no funds. While I was serving time at the Benton Work Release Center, there was quite a shake-up. The warden of the center was charged with a

DWI in Texarkana. This, by itself, was not that big a deal, but there also happened to be a naked, minor girl in the car, too. The warden might have even survived this unfortunate situation; however, the fact that he was on parole from an Illinois penitentiary where he had been held on a bank robbery charge was the straw that broke the camel's back. Several interim wardens were assigned to the center. The last one, who was there prior to my release in December 1978, was a man I got along with well, Rodney Nevens. Rodney had given me his card when I was paroled and told me that he would be going into private practice as an attorney in a few months. He told me to give him a call if I ever needed any help.

I called Debbie, and Debbie called Rodney. She found a job, paid Rodney a small retainer, and worked out a payment plan. I had an attorney and boy, what an attorney!

CHAPTER SEVEN

"Now, About This Robbery?"

Weapons are instruments of fear; they are not a wise man's tools.
He uses them only when he has no choice.
Peace and quiet are dear to his heart,
And victory no cause for rejoicing,
If you rejoice in victory, then you delight in killing;
If you delight in killing, you cannot fulfill yourself.

WRIGHTSVILLE UNIT

"Oh, yeah, Rodney did a hell of a job," I told Ted Brown, who was the single biggest factor in me abandoning my racial prejudice. As a black man, Ted used to be a source of amazement to me. He is intelligent, well spoken, quiet, and a veteran medical helicopter pilot of the Vietnam War. After reading his manuscript titled Dustoff *Three-One,* I was forced to admit: here was a black man I respected. Over the years we have spent together at Wrightsville, Ted and I have developed a strong friendship.

"You ought to write a book about this," suggested Ted.

"I started one when I was in the Dallas County Jail in 1984. I was writing in long hand and mailing it to Debbie, who typed it and sent it back to me. I had one hundred and sixty-seven typed pages completed before I was extradited to Tennessee. I thought I better send it back to her. Going up there to face a drug store robbery charge and carrying a book titled, *Speed Trap,* well; I didn't think it was such a good idea."

"What happened to it?" asked Ted.

"I have no idea. Probably wound up in the trash after Debbie and I divorced."

"Then start it again. This time you won't need anyone to type it for you," encouraged Ted.

I considered his suggestion. In my earlier attempt to write this story, I had been a completely different person. Back in 1984, I was all about glorifying my illegal activities and the story reflected that theme. In 1994, I feel quite differently about my exploits. It is impossible to feel glory over something that has had me incarcerated for fifteen of the thirty-eight years of my life.

"If I did, it would have to be in a way which told the truth about all that crap. It would have to be something which could be used to help keep kids from encountering the nightmare I have lived," I told Ted.

"You could do that!" offered my friend, sitting up on his bed, the gleam of excitement lighting his dark eyes.

The more I thought about it, the better the idea seemed. My job in Braille allowed me some free time and the use of a computer. I had already written one book in the project. A book about a fantasy land called Land's End titled, *The Cure of the Land*. The book is about four little girls, my nieces, who find their way to this magical land. Land's End is a troubled place, besieged by a realm to the south called Addiction. Addiction is controlled by a wicked witch, Mary Jane, and her evil henchmen, the twin trolls, Crack and Smack. The girls, with the aid of magic ruby rings given them by their Uncle Bill, help cure the land and destroy the witch. I had written the book for my four nieces and had just given it to them, along with ruby rings, last Christmas.

"You're right, I can do that! I'll start tomorrow," I exclaimed. Ted's excitement was infectious.

"Now that is settled, tell me what happened with this robbery charge," inquired Ted.

"Well, Rodney Nevens came to see me in jail..."

✗ ✗ ✗

"Good morning, Bill," said Rodney, as I entered the small attorney visiting room in the Pulaski County Jail.

"Morning," I responded. The concept of it being a "good" morning escaped me; although it was good to see Rodney.

I pulled a blue, plastic chair out and joined him at the wooden table where he was sitting. Rodney reached down, picked up his briefcase off the floor, and, laying it on the table, extracted a yellow legal tablet. Rodney is a large man with a deep and gruff voice. That I was one of his first cases after entering private practice did not bother me at all. I had a theory concerning Rodney that I am hesitant to put forth in this writing because he provided such a big service for me and acted in all details as a professional and friend. My theory was that while in law school, Rodney was so large that he was not out spending his nights chasing girls but in his room studying, forging his skills as an attorney. Whether this harsh and insensitive theory is correct, I have no idea; all I do know is that Rodney Nevens is a splendid attorney and assisted me well.

"Have you been served the green warrant from your parole officer?" he asked.

"Yes, well, he said he was my parole officer now. A guy named Bob Harper. He said Valery Weston is no longer with the parole department," I answered, pulling from my orange jumpsuit a copy of the warrant and handing it to him.

"Valery Weston? She was your parole officer when you left Arkansas?"

"Yes."

Rodney reviewed the paperwork I had given him and said, "Looks like you have problems with this, Bill."

"Yeah, I don't see how I can beat the not working and being out of the state charges, but the not reporting charge, I think I can beat that one."

"How's that?" asked Rodney.

"Ms. Weston told me that I didn't have to report anymore."

"Then we will call her as a witness. I really don't see how it will help though; they are going to nail you on the other two charges. Now, about this robbery?"

I proceeded to tell Rodney a distorted client/attorney version of my story, which was a careful blend of truth, innuendo, and outright lies. I had learned early in my criminal life that you do not tell your attorney you are guilty. They do not want to know if they are planning to take the case to trial. On the other hand, I did not waste his time either by attempting to profess my innocence.

Rodney was not so naive as to accept my version of the story as the truth, the whole truth, so help me God, either. He made an occasional note on his legal tablet and, after about twenty minutes, was ready to depart.

"Ok, Bill, that's enough for me to get started. I will file a motion for discovery today, and we will see what evidence they have. Your parole revocation hearing is scheduled for next Thursday. I will request that Valery Weston be there. I'll be back after I get discovery. You need anything?"

"No, thanks. Debbie is looking out for me," I answered as I stood and offered my hand. "Thanks, Rodney."

We shook hands, and he left, while I returned to my cell with my thoughts. I was resigned to the fact that I was going to have to do at least a six-month parole violation in prison, but I still felt like I could walk on the robbery. Just how wrong I was, I would soon find out.

✗ ✗ ✗

"Are you William Wade Allen?"

"Yes, sir."

"Allen, this is a parole revocation hearing. My name is Melvin Gray. I am the hearing examiner."

We were in a small meeting room at the jail and seated at the table with the hearing examiner were Rodney Nevens, my new parole officer, Bob Harper, and myself. Mr. Gray droned on and on about the violations I faced and finally asked me how I wished to plead.

Rodney spoke up on my behalf, "Not guilty."

The hearing examiner then turned to my parole officer and asked him to present his case.

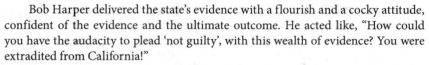

Bob Harper delivered the state's evidence with a flourish and a cocky attitude, confident of the evidence and the ultimate outcome. He acted like, "How could you have the audacity to plead 'not guilty', with this wealth of evidence? You were extradited from California!"

At the close of Harper's presentation, the examiner asked my attorney what he would like to present in rebuttal.

Rodney leaned back in his chair, crossed his arms across his considerable girth, and answered in his deep voice, "Mr. Gray, I have requested that Valery Weston be present for this hearing, however, I don't see her here."

"She is no longer with the parole division and was unavailable," interjected Harper.

"Well, that being the case, I must move that the allegations against Mr. Allen be dismissed."

"What do you base this conclusion on?" asked the examiner.

"Ms. Weston was Mr. Allen's parole officer in January of this year, and it is her name on the green warrant charging Mr. Allen with these violations. The defendant has the right to cross-examine the person bringing charges against him," responded my worthy attorney.

"Yes, I see what you mean," answered the examiner. "Mr. Harper, it was your duty to see that Ms. Weston was here. Do you have any response?"

"Yes, I, er, well, he, you know, well ... No!"

"Then it is my finding that William Allen is not guilty of these violations. Good day, gentlemen."

I could not believe it! Just like that and we won! The most difficult, albeit not the most serious of my charges, were history. I jumped up from my seat and shook Rodney's hand, pumping it effusively up and down saying, "Man that was great!"

Rodney took it all in stride; the only outward sign of his pleasure was a lifting of the corners of his mouth that barely evaded a smile. I think he took more pleasure beating the cocky Bob Harper, than he did keeping me out of prison for six months. He told me, "I will be over to see you later; I have the discovery file. We need to talk."

"Ok, whatever. Man, that was good. Did you hear him? 'er, yes, well, er ... No!'" I started laughing as Bob Harper turned and shot me a stare that made me glad that looks could not kill. I had made an enemy. Screw it. I did not care.

Later, when I met again with Rodney, he told me what the discovery file contained.

Bobby, Pete, and Pam had all signed statements telling pretty accurately what had transpired on the day of the robbery. The pharmacist was unable to identify me as the robber but had identified the drugs found in the sack. No fingerprints were found. The gun was registered to Bobby's dad, and my mother had told the police, when they questioned her, that the shirt found in the bag with the ski mask was a shirt my brother, Jason, had given me for Christmas.

The only part of this that surprised me was what my mother said. Not that she said it, but I just never considered the police questioning her.

"How can she identify that shirt?" I asked Rodney.

"Said she recognized it. I don't know."

"I will talk to her," I told him.

We talked for a while, considering and rejecting possible defenses. We finally settled on what we both believed would be the best course of action. Rodney left it to me to call my mom.

✗ ✗ ✗

"W. Allen, you have a visit," yelled the guard from the control booth.

I walked from my cell, which was actually a room, one of thirty in the pod where I lived, and waited for my escort to the visitation room.

As I approached my mother, I had a queer feeling in my stomach. It was difficult to face her. I thought back to the first time I was arrested, and my parents came to the jail to see me. I was only sixteen and was charged with minor in possession of alcohol, possession of a controlled substance, and possession of marijuana. A North Little Rock police sergeant, who knew my family, brought me upstairs to the detective's office. When I walked in, my mom was crying and said, "They tell me you have needle marks on your arms." My stoic father stood at her side, his arms crossed, already preparing to push me out of his life.

I do not know what it was that set me off so badly then, maybe the tears, maybe my guilt. Whatever it was, I was suddenly very angry and lashed out, "You want something to cry about, here look at this!"

I shoved the sleeve up my left arm, revealing needle marks running from wrist to elbow, complete with bruises from abscesses. It was not a pretty sight. The sergeant grabbed me by my collar and drug me from the room, cussing me as he hauled me back to my cell.

This time, however, my mother was not crying and I was not hostile. She stood up and received my hug and kiss on the cheek. "Hi, Mom."

"You are in real trouble now. They are talking about giving you a life sentence."

"They have to convict me first, Mom, and they aren't going to be able to do that," I responded, very confident now that I had beat the parole violations.

"Bill, the police have your shirt."

"What do you mean, 'my shirt'?"

"The red flannel shirt Jason gave you."

"Now, Mom, how can you say that is my shirt? Does it have any distinguishing marks on it? A laundry mark? My name sewed in it?"

"No, but I know it is your shirt."

"Could you swear under oath to that? Do you know how many shirts there are like that in Little Rock? Think about it, Mom. There is no way you could."

"No, now that you put it that way, I don't guess I could."

"That is what you need to tell the police when they ask you to testify at my trial. If you do that Mom, I'll beat this charge."

I had convinced her; I could see it in her eyes. She was not going to be the one to bring about my conviction with her testimony.

CHAPTER EIGHT

Confused and Scared

The world is ruled by letting things take their course.

"All rise! The Sixth Circuit Court of Pulaski County is now in session, the honorable Lyle Henderson presiding," stated the court bailiff as a brown, wooden door behind the raised bench of the judge opened and in walked Judge Lyle Henderson dressed in a long, flowing, black robe.

I stood beside Rodney at the defendant's table, dressed for the first time in over six months in something besides the bright orange jumpsuit, which is prisoner's fare at the Pulaski County Jail. I wore a three-piece suit that Debbie had purchased for me just for the occasion. I felt the heavy scrutiny of the focused attention of the courtroom since I was the reason for everyone's appearance here today.

Debbie did not attend the trial; unfortunately, her appearance would not be helpful at this point. I intentionally had her out of pocket because the only side she could aid was the one across the aisle. Our whole strategy relied upon the notion that, other than accomplices' testimony, there was no evidence to corroborate their statements. Debbie could easily provide that corroboration, and that was the last thing she or I wanted.

I had read many books concerning the jury selection process, voir dire. Like the characters in these books, I wanted the perfect jury. However, I was disappointed to find that for my trial the process only took two hours, and, before I knew it, the prosecutor was into his opening statement.

"Ladies and gentlemen of the jury, the case you are here to decide today is one of the easiest decisions you will have to ever make as to the guilt of the defendant in any case you happen to sit on as a member of a jury. I know that it is one of the most open and shut cases I have ever prosecuted. The State will show that the defendant William Wade Allen," thus saying the prosecutor turned and pointed at me, "armed with a twenty-two caliber, automatic pistol walked into Lyons Pharmacy at 4214 MacArthur Drive in North Little Rock on January 12 and robbed it of all its Schedule Two drugs. The defendant then exited the store through a side door and entered a car driven by an accomplice to make his getaway. The evidence will also show that the accomplice exited the getaway car at Parkway Village Apartments carrying the stolen drugs, the ski mask worn by the defendant, and the gun used in the robbery and abandoned them under a stairwell at the apartments. These items were found by an off duty Pulaski County Deputy who doubles as a security guard at the apartments. These items were subsequently turned over to the North Little Rock Police Department and that registration of the pistol was found to be to a Jeffrey Alan Futch at 3456 Kiehl Avenue."

"The State will prove that further investigation led to Bobby Alan Futch, who in fact, was the driver of the getaway car and who will testify to the involvement of the defendant William Wade Allen."

"At the conclusion of the State's case, there will not only be no reasonable doubt as to the fact that William Wade Allen perpetrated the aggravated robbery of Lyons Pharmacy, but there will be no doubt whatsoever."

Closing with that little bit of flourish, the prosecutor pointed at me and then took his seat at the prosecution table. I was sitting beside Rodney unsuccessfully trying to look innocent of the charges the prosecutor had hurled at me. I gazed around the room as if I did not have a care in the world, bold enough even to make eye contact with several jury members and shake my head as if to say, "Don't believe a word he says." Rodney straightened some papers in front of him and then rose to begin our opening statement.

Walking straight to the jury section, he stood before them and opened with, "Remember what the prosecutor told you the State was going to prove to you, and I quote, 'there will not only be no reasonable doubt as to the fact that William Wade Allen perpetrated the aggravated robbery of Lyons Pharmacy, but there will be no doubt whatsoever.'

"Well, there is no doubt that Lyons Pharmacy was held up at gun point. There is also no doubt that the police were able to come up with a suspect. Through their initial investigation, they found out that Bobby Futch was the son of the owner of the gun allegedly used in the robbery. But, ladies and gentlemen of the jury, there is doubt as to the validity of any statements or accusations made by the prime suspect in this case."

"I am confident that by following closely the sequence of events and by paying close attention to the witnesses the State puts on and what they have to gain or lose through their testimony, you will end up just as doubtful as I am as to any involvement of Bill Allen."

Rodney's speech raised my spirits somewhat, but I saw enough doubt in the jury's eyes that I was still scared to death.

"Thank you, gentlemen," said the judge. "Mr. Prosecutor, is the State ready to call your first witness?"

The prosecutor stood and answered, "Yes, Your Honor. The State calls Bobby Futch."

The door at the back of the courtroom opened and in walked my partner,

Bobby. Gone was the waist length hair, and he looked just like any neighborhood, clean-cut, young man. Bobby made his way down the courtroom aisle and through the little batwing doors that separate the court spectators from those participating in the trial. He walked directly to the witness stand where the bailiff, who held out a Bible, met him and raising his right hand asked Bobby, "Do you swear to tell the truth, the whole truth, so help you God?"

Bobby, after placing his left hand on the Bible and raising his right hand, answered, "I do."

My former partner then took a seat in the witness chair as the prosecutor approached him and directed him to state his name for the Court.

"Robert Alan Futch."

"Mr. Futch, do you recall what you were doing on January 12 of this year?"

"Yes, I do."

"Would you please tell the Court in your own words what all transpired that day."

"Sure."

This began a recounting of that fateful day which culminated in Bobby losing all of the proceeds of the robbery. It was very difficult to sit there and listen to this former friend of mine tell the entire world the events of a day which I would never dream of revealing to anyone. I was forced to sit there and listen to the perpetration of the biggest taboo it had ever been my personal horror to witness ... a friend testifying against a friend, a betrayal I did not condone, yet could understand.

Bobby's story went pretty much along the factual line. But when he reached the point of me coming from the robbery and getting in the car, Bobby went a step too far.

"And Bill opened the passenger door and pushed the bucket seat forward and climbed in the back seat and demanded that I drive. As I was pulling out of the parking lot, I felt a pressure against the back of my head and turned to see Bill with the gun barrel right against my head."

"I asked him, 'What's up?' and he responded, 'I have been to prison once, and I am not going back; if you stop for any reason, I will kill you!'"

I almost shot from my chair and called him a liar. Rodney reached over and grabbed my arm to prevent me from any rash action; he then rose and voiced an objection. I could not believe what this perjurer was saying. He was pretending that the story I had told him about what I had done with Henry after the Blake robbery was what transpired during the Lyons robbery. However, it was not the fact of his lie that prompted my attorney to object, it was the information which the State's witness revealed to the jury.

"Your honor, I move for a mistrial. May I approach the bench?"

"Yes, attorney's for the State and defense approach," answered Judge Henderson.

Rodney and the prosecutor both approached the bench as I sat there glaring at Bobby. I was rewarded with him casting a quick glance at me. In that single look, I was pouring out every ounce of hate that I felt for this snitching and lying, so-called friend. He quickly diverted his gaze to escape my glare.

I could not hear what was taking place in the conference at the bench; however, it did not last long. Rodney turned and walked quickly back to our table with a smile on his face while the prosecutor slowly returned to his place looking like he had been sucking on a lemon.

"What's up?" I asked Rodney.

"The judge is granting a mistrial."

"Why?" I did not know if I was supposed to be happy or not. Did this mean that there would be a second trial, or was it over? "What does this mean?" I whispered to Rodney.

"Hold on, I'll tell you in a minute."

"Ladies and gentlemen of the jury, I am granting the defendant's motion for a mistrial. The prosecution has committed a fatal error. They allowed their witness to reveal to you that the defendant has a felony conviction by the witness' testimony concerning the defendant's statement that he had been in prison before. You are dismissed. This Court is adjourned." So saying, the judge rose and exited through the door behind his bench.

The bailiff and a Pulaski County police officer that had transported me from the jail to the courthouse approached, and Rodney asked them for a minute to confer with his client.

"Bill, this means that they will try you again. You'll have to return to the jail, and I will let you know as soon as possible when your next trial will be."

"Crap!" I responded. I wanted to go home! Out of all the possible outcomes of this trial, I never considered the possibility of a mistrial. One way or another, I had expected this to be over today.

"Bill, we couldn't allow them to get away with prejudicing the jury against you with the knowledge that you have a felony record serious enough for you to have gone to prison."

"Yeah, you're right. Good job, Rodney. Let me know something as soon as you can."

Rodney then nodded at the bailiff and cop, and they returned me to the jail.

X   X   X

"All rise! The Sixth Circuit Court of Pulaski County is now in session, the honorable Lyle Henderson presiding," stated the court bailiff once again. A little over a month had passed since my mistrial. Here we were again.

Everything progressed just as the other trial with the exception that Bobby did not make any statements about my prior incarceration or tell any lies about me putting a gun to his head. As a matter of fact, Bobby cooperated with our strategy as much as any friend snitching on a friend could. Prior to this trial, attorneys for Pete Battles and Bobby asked Rodney if there was anything that their clients could do at this late a point to minimize their damage to me. Kind of late to be concerned about my well being, I thought, but Rodney told them the best thing they could do for me at this late juncture was to tell the truth. As a last act of consolation, they did.

The entire prosecution's case relied on Pam Battles' testimony. They knew that the pharmacist could not identify me as the robber. Also, there were no fingerprints or physical evidence that could link me to the robbery. They realized that Bobby and Pete were accomplices, and that their testimony alone could not convict me. What they needed was someone's description of the events that would support or corroborate their testimonies. Pam Battles fit the bill perfectly.

After Bobby's testimony, the prosecutor put the pharmacist of Lyons Drug on the stand, and he told his side of what occurred that day in January. The prosecutor then took a box and asked that its contents be entered into evidence as State's Exhibit #1. Inside the box were all the drugs that I had taken from the pharmacy and that Bobby had subsequently abandoned beneath a stairwell at Parkway Village Apartments. The prosecutor asked the pharmacist if he could identify the bottles of drugs, which he did by pulling them from the box one bottle at a time and setting them on the rail which fronted and ran along the sides of the witness stand. This rail was about four inches wide and, by the time the pharmacist finished his inspection, it was filled with bottles. This impacted me deeply as I sat there watching him do his inspection and take inventory. I could identify each different drug by the shape and color of the bottles, and I did a mental inventory of the street value of the dope. I was astounded and hated Bobby more at that moment than I ever had. This was the biggest score I had ever achieved. Had Bobby just done as planned, we would have gotten away with it.

The next witness was the police officer who first arrived at the pharmacy and then the security officer who had found the sack of dope, gun, and ski mask, which he promptly identified. Next up was the chief detective of the case. He testified about his investigation, the subsequent arrest of Bobby and questioning of Pete and Pam Battles. None of this testimony was in the least bit damaging to me. Nothing that was said could pin me down.

After this string of useless testimony, Pete's turn on the stand arrived. Pete told of my arrival at his house the morning of the robbery and of us driving around looking for, and finally finding Lyons and deciding that it would be the ultimate target. Pete testified about our agreement that he would provide a vehicle for us to use as a switch car after the robbery and how he would be the one to sell my drugs for me. He continued with how Bobby returned to his house after the robbery, my late arrival, and everything that transpired. Pete never deviated from the truth. He neither embellished nor tried to make it seem less than it was. It was a robbery, and he was deeply involved. Though, he had nothing to fear because the State had already granted Pam and him immunity from prosecution for their testimony.

The deciding moment of the trial arrived as Pam took her oath. Up until this point, Rodney's cross-examination of the State's witnesses had been circumscribed.

Pam rehashed my arrival at their house on that fateful day, of her anger at her husband for allowing me there, and of her fear of his involvement with me. She explained that she was aware of my activities, and she did not want Pete to get into trouble. She testified that she was excluded from our planning, but at one point she saw a ski mask and in her heart knew what was going to happen. Continuing with her testimony, she recounted the events at her house after the robbery, and then the prosecutor ended by stating, "No further questions of this witness. The State closes."

The Prosecutor felt that he had done his job; Pam's testimony linked me to the robbery through a witness who was not involved. Confidence radiated from him as he took his seat. Rodney rose to question Pam.

"Mrs. Battles, I have just a few questions for you. First off, prior to the robbery, did you know a robbery was going to take place?"

"No, not really I mean, I knew that with Bill Allen ... well I knew what he does. He robs drug stores. But no, I wasn't in on their plans."

"Ok, that's fine. How about after the robbery? Did you know that a robbery had been committed?"

"Yes, I knew for sure then."

"Mrs. Battles, did you call the police and report a robbery?" asked Rodney.

"Why, no," Pam answered.

With her answer, Rodney turned to the judge and announced, "Your Honor, I move for a directed verdict. The State has closed its case and has failed in its burden of proof. There is absolutely no evidence linking the defendant to the robbery other than accomplices' testimony. Clearly, Bobby Futch and Pete Battles are accomplices, and Pam Battles is an admitted accomplice by her testimony that she knew that a robbery, a felony, had been committed and that she did not call the police to report it. That makes her an accomplice!"

The judge leaned back in his chair, crossed his arms, and just looked at Rodney while the prosecutor jumped from his chair and started in on his argument denying Rodney's claim that Pam Battles was an accomplice. The judge just stared at Rodney and then turned his stare toward me. I was sitting on the edge of my seat, my heart in my throat. This was it; this was the whole ball of wax. The judge's decision would make or break me.

"We will adjourn to my chambers." So saying, the judge stood and exited through the door behind the bench, followed by a smiling Rodney and an angry prosecutor.

They were gone for about ten minutes while I tried unsuccessfully to control my excitement and anxiety, both of which drove me to the limits of what I could endure. When they returned to the courtroom, Rodney led the way with a big grin on his face. My eyes were only for him, looking to read the result of the meeting in the judge's chamber.

"Well?" I asked as Rodney arrived at our table.

"The judge is going to direct a verdict of acquittal, Bill. We did it! We win!"

I was just barely able to restrain myself from jumping up and dancing on the table.

"Ladies and gentlemen of the jury," began the judge. "You have spent the entire day listening to the testimony in this court, and I know that you all believe, just as I do, in the guilt of the defendant. Therefore, I feel that I owe you an explanation of why I am fixing to let a guilty man go free. There are laws that insure that all defendants receive a fair trial. One of those laws states that a defendant cannot be convicted solely on accomplices' testimony. This law requires that there must be corroborating evidence that supports accomplices' testimony. This insures that an innocent defendant will not be convicted upon the testimony of those who have the most to gain from their testament. In this case, we have three accomplices who have all gained from their testimony against William Allen. Bobby Futch has pleaded guilty to his involvement in this crime and has agreed to testify for a promised minimal sentence of five years in prison. Pete and Pam Battles agreed to testify under an agreement of immunity. Clearly, these witnesses profit from their testimony and it is only through their testimony that the defendant is linked to this crime. Therefore, I am entering in a directed verdict of acquittal of the defendant and am ordering him to be released from custody."

I jumped up and hugged Rodney. The judge spoke again, this time looking at me, "Not so fast, young man."

Then, he looked out in the court room, located Bobby, and said, "Mr. Futch, approach the bench."

Bobby, looking confused and scared walked forward and stood before the judge.

"Mr. Futch, you have pleaded guilty to the crime of aggravated robbery, and sentencing has been delayed until after your testimony in this trial. I could not live with myself if I were to sentence you to prison when you have testified in behalf of the State and were only the driver in this robbery while the man who went inside and committed the actual robbery armed with a gun, goes free. I am hereby going to defer sentencing on you for the period of five years. If you stay out of trouble, your record will remain clean."

"Now, Mr. Allen, you will be returned to the jail and then processed out. You are free. However, I want to warn you. If I ever hear of any retribution towards Mr. Futch or the Battles', I will personally see to it that you are placed in the penitentiary. Do you understand me?"

Too excited to be phased by this threat, I simply answered, "Yes, sir."

CHAPTER NINE

Pulling Her Closer to Me

There is no greater sin than desire,
No greater curse than discontent,
No greater misfortune than wanting something for oneself.
Therefore he who knows that enough is enough will always have enough.

After my acquittal, the road to the future lay open before me, yet I lacked the vision to see the way. Having already completed the pre-marriage requirement of a blood test, Debbie and I returned to the courthouse the next day to acquire our marriage license.

After receiving directions, we boarded an elevator to take us to the correct floor. Unlikely as it would seem, one of our fellow passengers on this elevator was the judge who presided over my recent trial, Judge Lyle Henderson.

Debbie, not having been present at the trial, failed to recognize him, but the judge's eyes and mine locked on each other immediately. As the elevator doors slowly slid shut, I said, "Good morning, Your Honor."

"William," was his single response.

I could not come to a conclusion in regards to his feelings about me with only his stoic expression as evidence. His eyes showed no emotion, and the corners of his mouth neither turned upward nor down, before, during, or after saying my name. It was an awkward moment and yet something compelled me to try to show this abnormality of the justice system, this fair arbiter, that he had made the correct decision by directing my acquittal.

"Your Honor, you know I was guilty," I acknowledged, having no fear now, secure in my knowledge that the double jeopardy clause of the U.S. Constitution barred a second trial.

"Yes, I am aware of that," he responded, his face carved in stone, still lacking even the slightest hint of emotion.

I was wholly oblivious of the other people on the elevator or of its transit towards our destination. I am not even sure if there were others on board. To me, the entire world consisted of my future wife and the man who allowed me that future.

My intentions were not to mock him or the system of laws that afforded me my freedom but to thank him in some small way and reassure him he had made the correct decision about me. Thus motivated, I continued, "I just want to thank you and to tell you that I am through with drugs and drug store robberies." Putting my arm around Debbie's shoulder and pulling her closer to me, I said, "This is my fiancée, Debbie, and we are here today to get our marriage license. I am going to get married, settle down, and go to work."

"Congratulations. I wish you both the best." Saying this, the man actually smiled and shook my hand. The elevator then stopped, the doors opened, and the honest, fair jurist was gone from my life. Today, as I sit in prison, I occasionally see television commercials advertising the *Lyle Henderson Law Firm*, and these advertisements never fail to elicit a reminiscence of that trial, the encounter on the elevator, and the fact that I blew the biggest break of my entire life.

The day after my jury trial, Debbie and I visited a Justice of the Peace in the Levy area of North Little Rock, Arkansas and were married. No church, no family, no well-wishers, no bridesmaids, no best man, and no wedding march ... none of the typical trimmings of a normal matrimonial celebration. These were only the first of many satisfactions that I denied Debbie throughout our married life. Nonetheless, on this day, my wife was happy, as was her husband.

We rented a small trailer just two blocks from Concord Boats in Sherwood, where I returned to work building ski boats. Debbie was working as a secretary for the Ideal Bread Company and married life was pleasurable for the first few months.

This phase was one of many times during my life when I was resolute I would get off drugs, quit robbing drug stores, and live a conventional life, one I had absolutely no idea how to live. My determination did not include a determination to stop drinking, smoking pot or running around with my old friends. Lacking that determination, all of my idealistic dreams were doomed. I was destined for catastrophe. Being dishonest with myself, I believed returning to my old behavior would somehow get different results.

All it took for my fragile resolve to crumble was for one of my old friends to show up with speed in his pocket.

Slightly over a year after Henry had decided it would be healthier to live elsewhere, he returned to my life. Leaving Concord during my lunch break to go drink a few bottles, I approached the old Ford Fairlane, a gift to Debbie from her grandmother. Hearing a horn honking nearby, I saw Henry parked a few cars down from mine. When I looked to see who was honking, Henry waved from the driver's window. A smile spread across my face as I recognized my old conspirator. My course was altered.

"What's up?" I asked as I reached for his hand and shook it. He remained sitting in his car.

"How ya doing, Bill, I heard you and Debbie got married."

"Who did you hear that from?" I asked.

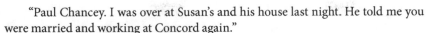

"Paul Chancey. I was over at Susan's and his house last night. He told me you were married and working at Concord again."

"Yeah. You know I beat that Lyons robbery," I boasted.

"Yes, I read about it in the paper. Way to go!"

"Yeah, well, Debbie and I got hitched the day after I beat that charge," I continued.

"Hey, man, hop in and show me your trailer. Paul said it was close by."

I glanced at my watch. I only had thirty minutes for lunch and though I was not punching a time clock, I did not want to cut it close. "Okay. Drive to the liquor store first, and I'll get us a six pack."

I walked around to the passenger side, opened the door and climbed inside. Before I could pull the door shut Henry held out his open hand and in his palm sat a small, yet bulging, square plastic package filled with an off-white crystalline powder. "You sure you want some beer?" Henry asked with a devilish grin on his face.

So much for that rickety old wagon I'd been riding on. I did not just fall off; I jumped off and never looked back! "Screw some beer!" I answered. With this single act, I began the long, spiraling fall that would not end until I was once again behind bars.

We drove to my trailer and once inside, I asked Henry, "What's in the package?" Although the question was rhetorical, I asked it anyway.

"Crank," was the one word, inevitable response.

Crank is a homemade speed. It is produced through a lengthy and complicated chemical process which requires great skill and certain knowledge. At that point in time in 1981, "meth labs" were not as widespread as they are now. Had they been and had crank been as readily accessible as it is now, it is almost guaranteed I would not have been robbing drug stores to support my habit. I probably would have been a bank robber instead, stealing money to support a slightly different monkey on my back.

"You got a rig?" I asked him, completely caught up with the thrill of being so close to such a long-awaited high. Yet, it was not just a high I sought. A high comes from smoking a joint or dropping a hit of acid. I was getting ready to receive "The Shot!"

There are two types of speed shooters: those who like to get "up" and those who like to get "down." I was of the latter persuasion; I did not shoot speed in order to get that "go-fast, euphoric, everything is wonderful with the world" feeling which the "up" shooters liked. When I shot speed, I wanted it to knock me on my ass, cross my eyes, and make it so I could not even speak. I wanted to "over-amp."

Over-amping is when your body realizes you have injected too much speed into it and it throws a circuit breaker. You get a rush that threatens to take you beyond the atmosphere. Your pulse quickly rises to an extraordinary rate. Then abruptly, right before it gets to be too much, just before your brain begins to fry, the switch is thrown, causing you to sink down as fast as you were flying high. Your pulse drops from one hundred and forty beats per minute to sixty in the blink of an eye. All your limbs turn to rubber. If you are standing, you fall. If you are sitting, you sink low in your chair. Your mouth and eyes refuse to work properly. Your eyes cross and drool seeps from your lips. And it feels great! *Scary*, but great! The first time you over-amp, you're sure you are going to die. Thereafter, if you *do not* over-amp, you feel you have wasted your time.

"The Shot" is what I sought every time I injected speed. It is the motivating force that allowed me to abandon all caution and enter a pharmacy with a gun in my hand. It was a monster which, once awakened, never gave me a moment's peace until it was sated. And it was a hungry bastard, exceedingly tough to satisfy.

Henry did not articulate a response to my obviously obtuse question. He just gave me a look that said, "Do you take me for a fool?" reached in his coat pocket and produced a handful of one cc syringes still in their paper and plastic wrappings. Without further ado, I went to the kitchen, opened a drawer, retrieved two large tablespoons, and set them on the kitchen table.

Henry pulled a chair from the table and sat down as I filled a glass with water. Thus armed, I joined him at the table.

Gone were all my past animosities with Henry. Gone was my sense of responsibility at work. Gone were my duties to my wife. Gone was my determination to stay clean. The only thing I was thinking about was that ugly monster, that all consuming bastard who demanded to be fed. Henry pulled from his pocket the plastic package, which was a small Ziploc bag and handed it to me.

"You go ahead and go first," he offered.

"How much does it take?" I asked as I opened the bag and started pouring some into the spoon that lay on the table.

"Quite a bit. It's not that pure."

"This stuff any good?" I questioned as the monster inside me wailed, suddenly anxious that he would not be fed.

"Oh, yeah, it's good. It's just bathtub crank, but it will knock your socks off if you do enough," promised Henry.

By this time, I had a small pile in my spoon, and I looked up at Henry questioningly.

"More," he prompted.

A couple more taps on the bag with my index finger doubled the amount in my spoon, and I looked at Henry again.

"A little more."

My doubts were escalating, and the monster's wails turned to whimpers as I realized that today was not going to be the day that I got "The Shot." At this point, I almost pushed the spoon over in front of Henry and returned the package of speed. Why waste my time and put my marriage and job in jeopardy for a shot of dope that was not going to get me where I wanted to be? I was not an experienced crank shooter, but the crank I had shot let me know if I had to do this much, it was not very good.

Henry must have read the doubt on my face as he said, "Trust me, a little more." I was not worried about doing too much; I did not think it was possible to overdo it with speed. I always felt like over-amping was a safety mechanism that refused to allow your body to react to lethal doses. Once the switch was thrown at the extreme limit of what you could endure, the remainder just floated harmlessly through your system. Whether this is factual, I cannot say. All I know is I have done ungodly amounts of speed, enough to knock me out and put me to sleep for hours, without dying. All I ever worried about was not getting "The Shot."

One more tap on the package with my finger finally caused Henry to say, "That should do it."

Still skeptical, I opened one of the syringe packages and twisted the plastic cap off the needle. Inserting the point into the glass of water, I filled it about half way.

"Don't use too much water on this, or you won't be able to get it all in the syringe. It has a tendency to grow," instructed Henry.

Following his counsel, I squirted about half of what I had pulled up back into the glass, then holding the needle over the spoon of dope, I slowly squirted some of the water on the pile of crank. As the water hit the off-white crystals and dissolved them, I took the cap that had covered the needle and started slowly stirring the mixture in the spoon. The result was a thick, brown, syrupy concoction that raised my doubts and skepticism to new levels.

Pure crank, when mixed with just a few drops of water, dissolves completely, and the water remains crystal clear. Even with the cut substance, the water remains virtually clear. There may be some residue which will not dissolve, the trash it is cut with, but this stuff was unprecedented in my experience. The pharmaceutical cocaine I used to shoot was so pure that I would not even go through the trouble of using a spoon or straining it through cotton. I used to just pull the plunger from the syringe and use a tiny coke spoon to pour a small quantity down the barrel of the rig. I would then put the plunger back in and push it down, compressing the dope and removing the air from the syringe and then insert the needle in a vein. This way, I just utilized my blood to break down the pure dope. But this crap, this brown, thick, barely fluid syrup … I looked at my watch and saw that twenty-five of my thirty-minute lunch break had already expired. What the hell, I decided. I added a little bit more water in hopes of thinning this syrup enough to allow it to flow through the needle.

Henry was right; this stuff did grow. My spoon was almost half full of fluid, and I knew there was no way I would be able to fit it all in a one cc syringe. "Do you have a three cc rig?" I asked him.

"No. But you'll be able to get more of that in a one cc than you think. What you do get should do ya," he answered with a smirk on his face.

"We'll see," I answered, ever the skeptic. I pulled a pack of Kool cigarettes from my shirt pocket and shook one from the pack. Breaking the filter off, I threw the tobacco half in the trashcan sitting in the corner of the room. I then tore the filter in half, length-wise, and pulled a long thin strip off from one of the halves. Taking the syringe in my right hand and the thin strip of cigarette filter in my left, I carefully inserted the needle through the center of the strip. This made a filter with which I could strain the soup in the spoon. I lowered the impromptu filter into the fluid, and, once it had absorbed some of the liquid, I started pulling the plunger back. This crap was so thick that this became a painstakingly tedious process.

"Man, is this gonna kill me?" I asked Henry, holding the thick, brown concoction up to the light and inspecting it.

"Nah, just don't miss any. An abscess from this stuff will really mess your arm up," Henry warned.

I was not aware at the time that this was the same stuff that caused Henry to lose his foot. He had told me that he shot cocaine into an artery in his foot, not this bathtub crank. I had never even heard of bathtub crank and, until this writing, never given any thought as to how it acquired its name. It is not made in a bathtub, although I guess some forms of homemade crank could be mixed in one.

Pulling the cotton off the needle, I inserted the needle in the glass of water to wash off any residue that was on it. I then laid the syringe on the table and proceeded to roll up my left sleeve. I presented my left arm to Henry to hold off and picked up the syringe. Henry took a secure grip around my upper biceps, completely cutting off the flow of blood and causing my veins to emerge. I pumped my arm a couple of times, forcing the veins to rise even further and then selecting my target, lowered the needle to a thick vein on the inside of my elbow. Placing the point right in the center of this vein, I pushed on the syringe, and it slipped into the vein. Pulling back on the plunger a fraction, I was rewarded with a strong stream of blood flowing into the syringe and mixing with the dope, proving I was securely within the vein. Without moving the needle any, I changed my grip on the syringe and used my index finger to push the plunger in, injecting the dope. As the plunger struck home, I reversed my grip and pulled the plunger back to "boot" the shot. Blood filled the syringe, and, changing my grip once again, I started shooting this blood, along with whatever dope it rinsed out of the syringe, back into my vein. Before I could even get the plunger back to the end, the rush started hitting me. It came with the vigor of a locomotive. I quickly pulled the rig from my arm and wiped off the drop of blood that flowed from the small puncture. I then dropped the rig on the floor as the monster that drove me was fed to the gills. My eyes crossed, and I slumped back in my chair, almost joining the syringe on the floor. My breath rushed out of me in a "whoosh." I swear I could see fumes that looked like the heat waves you see rising from a blacktop highway on a summer day.

The monster was momentarily satisfied. I could not even verbalize my gratitude to Henry. As he reached for the package of speed, he said, "Told ya!"

Needless to say, boat building was postponed. Henry and I spent the afternoon shooting the remainder of his crank. I give this one afternoon such attention through these pages because it played such a principal role as a major stumbling block in my life. During this afternoon, not only did I fall from my short wagon trip, I learned a simple method of making the cheap crank Henry and I had been shooting. Even though I do not think the ingredients are obtainable in the free world any longer, I will not detail that recipe in this narrative.

Looking at my watch, I exclaimed, "Damn, it is almost five o'clock! I've got to pick up Debbie from work."

"Want me to take you? I'd like to see Debbie," asked Henry.

"No, I don't think that would be a good idea. She's going to be pissed at me for doing this speed, and it would probably be better if you weren't around. Just take me back to Concord so I can get our car."

While driving to the boat company, Henry asked, "What are you going to be doing tomorrow? You gotta work?"

The next day found that hungry bastard of a monster perched upon my shoulder demanding to be fed once again. I had hardly slept all night, struggling with the speed still in my system, and had Debbie call my boss at Concord and tell him I was sick. I stayed in bed until I heard Debbie drive off, and then I was up and anxiously awaiting Henry's appearance.

Finally Henry arrived and I was out the door in a flash. Opening his car door and climbing in I demanded, "What took you so long?"

"Sorry, man. I overslept."

It was past eleven and to me, half the day was gone. I had had too many hours alone with my conscience and wanted to get the show on the road. Being busy was the best way I knew to quiet that small voice which was constantly reminding me just how far I was falling.

"What's the plan?" I asked.

"We need to pick up some inhalers. I already have everything else. You got any money? The inhalers will cost about three dollars apiece, and we will need at least six of them."

"Yeah, I have about twenty bucks, but, if I spend all of it, Debbie would be so pissed. I can go ten dollars, but that's all I can spare," I answered.

"That's cool. I've got the rest," offered Henry as we drove from the trailer park.

We purchased the inhalers from a pharmacy on Kiehl Avenue in Sherwood just a few blocks away and then returned to my trailer.

"Do they have any idea what these things can be used for?" I questioned Henry, while examining one of the packaged inhalers, reading the active ingredients.

"Yeah, they know. Couldn't you tell with the way that pharmacist looked at us?"

"That's what I thought. He better watch out, or I'll come rob him!" I said, only half jokingly.

The remnants of the day were spent feeding the monster, and then it was time to face the music as Debbie returned home.

CHAPTER TEN

My Usual Despicable Behavior

Keep your mouth shut, guard the senses, and life is ever full.
Open your mouth, always be busy, and life is beyond hope.

WRIGHTSVILLE UNIT

As I paused in recounting my story, Ted leaned back on the bed. Even though his thoughts were translated through his eyes, he did me the benefit of verbalizing them.

"Man, that sucks! That really sucks! Debbie held her mud through all those interrogations, visited you every week, hired you an attorney, married you, and you go back on that crap, totally screwing her around. That really sucks!"

I had no defense against Ted's legitimate attack on my behavior. My actions were wholly reproachable. It really *did* suck! I spread my arms, palms upturned in a gesture that said, "What can I say?" Ted just shook his head, and I said, "I never have believed that I got this fifty year sentence with no parole for a single drug store robbery. I believe that the "karma counter of life" finally became so unbalanced in my life, all the chances I had been given, all the opportunities I had, all the people I hurt, all came crashing down upon me in one fell swoop."

The sentence I had been given was disproportionate to those given to other robbers. I have seen many murderers and rapists come and go since I have been incarcerated. Couple the fifty year sentence given for one robbery, with the no parole restriction, a stricture usually placed on four-time losers, not two-time losers like me, and you come up with a karmic slap in the face that says, "It's time for you to pay, boy!"

"Chow call!" yelled the guard.

"Come on, let's go eat," said Ted. "We have established how big a piece of crap you are, or at least were, and you can finish elaborating on the theme when we return."

It was a pretty day, clear sky with a light breeze blowing softly from the south, as Ted and I walked the back road around the compound, taking the scenic route. As we strolled we encountered many people from different barracks going to and returning from the chow hall. As we passed each other, I began to discern how many of the inmates spoke to Ted. They offered greetings in casual ways, "What's up, Ted?" or "How ya doing man?" and Ted always responded in his cheerful manner, "Not much." or "How are you?"

During our trip to and from the chow hall, I probably witnessed twenty-five or thirty of these exchanges, and it really struck home just how anti-social I had become. What had happened to the person who could get along in any group? The person who used to like to say, "I meet no strangers." Had my years in prison altered me so much that I could walk amid a group of two hundred people and not once speak to anyone or vice versa? Apparently, it had.

Through my involvement with the Wrightsville Braille project, I was learning the benefit of giving without any concern for what would be gained in return, discovering that the simple act of charity brought its own rewards. Yet, this walk with Ted showed me that regardless of how much had changed from the gun-toting, drugstore Bill, I still had a long road ahead of me in order to abandon my old convict behaviors so that I would fit in polite society.

After returning from chow, Ted brought us back to where I had left off in my tale. "So, was Debbie upset with you when you picked her up?"

"Very much so. But that was just a drop in the bucket to what she was to face in the very near future."

✗ ✗ ✗

Thus, I started a futile attempt to juggle my responsibilities: my responsibilities to my wife, to my job, and the newest and toughest responsibility of all - to feed that ever-desirous, hungry monster.

After climbing in the car, all it took was one look at my eyes for Debbie to know I was wired. She dealt me the silent treatment all the way home even though I broached a mundane topic or two for conversation.

When we got home, resorting to my usual despicable behavior when I'm wrong, I blew up. I used my temper to intimidate her.

"What the hell is your problem?" I screamed, throwing my keys at her and slamming the trailer door.

Her tears started immediately, which only enraged me more. "Bill, you promised you were through with drugs," Debbie pleaded.

"I did not! I promised I wouldn't rob any more drug stores. Have I robbed one? Huh? have I?"

"I don't know, have you?"

"No! I haven't robbed any drug stores. Is that what you want? You want me to get Henry and rob one?" I taunted.

I watched the fear grow in her eyes and I knew I would win this battle. Knowing it would not be starved, the monster within me swelled at the victory.

"If this is what I have to put up with just for doing a shot of free dope, I might as well be robbing stores." I stomped around the den for a minute as Debbie watched, probably wondering how someone she loved so much could be such an idiot and yet vowing not to push me over the edge, this or any other time. Unfortunately, I was already over the brink, falling off a lofty cliff. It just took a while for me to strike bottom.

Retrieving my keys from the floor, I stormed from the trailer and drove off. From the car, I saw Debbie observe me from the kitchen window, watching her husband disappear to an unknown location. However, even with my threats, I was not close to robbing another store. I had found a source for my habit which I knew I could utilize without reaching that extreme.

I went to the liquor store, purchased a quart of beer, and returned home. I had already won this battle, and now it was time for peace. I still had a lot of juggling to do.

Debbie was so happy to see me return that she totally capitulated in our earlier confrontation. If I were to pinpoint one shortcoming with my new and beautiful bride, it would be that she gave in too easily. Yet, I cannot even in all honesty say that was a failing. It probably saved her from her abusive and sometimes totally out-of-control husband.

I sat in the den, drinking a glass of beer as I rolled a joint and Debbie fixed supper in the kitchen. My rolling task accomplished, I fired the joint and went into the kitchen. Debbie had her back to me working at the stove. I approached and tapped her on the shoulder, offering her the burning joint. She turned her head far enough to see my offering but shook it to indicate that although she had capitulated, there was still some ice to melt before my warm and loving wife would be magnanimous toward me.

I placed the joint lighted end in my mouth, grasped Debbie with both hands on her shoulders, and gently turned her to face me, forcefully enough to overcome her initial resistance. My right hand slid up under the back of her blouse while my left pulled her head towards mine as I blew her a shotgun off the joint in my mouth. The smoke shot out in a full, strong stream and after just a second of futile defiance, Debbie opened her mouth and, unlike our former president and fellow Arkansan, inhaled the smoke deep into her lungs.

Holding her breath as I removed the joint from my mouth, Debbie stared deep into my eyes. I could read love, mistrust, fear and doubt all at the same time in her entrancing eyes. I winked and with her exhalation of the marijuana smoke, the remaining frost thawed. She pulled me to her and held me tight in her arms.

We ate supper, smoked another joint and eventually went to bed where we had one of our "after the fight" lovemaking sessions, which were generally the most impassioned. Tonight was no exception.

We awoke in the morning and after making love again we went to work. Life settled back into a false sense of normalcy that was in reality only a slight lull before the storm. The monster was awakened and always made it's presence known. Although

I did not give in to it all the time, neither did I deny the monster some joy. I had learned a cheap and swift way to manufacture this bathtub crank. The juggling act was on as I attempted to balance my desires with my responsibilities; the balancing was accomplished only through lies and pretext. Sometimes I would let Debbie know what I was doing and cook the dope in front of her. Oftentimes, I would sneak about like a child hiding a cigarette from his parents. I was on straight salary at Concord and put in enough hours so that my boss did not complain. The salary hid the fact that sometimes when Debbie thought I was at work I was actually out cooking and shooting dope. The fact that I was able to accomplish this, at least to a degree, spoke volumes of my growing skill to manage the Jekyll and Hyde within me.

With two paychecks coming in week after week, Debbie and I decided that we could afford better accommodations. This we did by locating a nice two-bedroom house in Jacksonville. It was only about two weeks after our move that my facade at work was penetrated.

One night while Debbie thought I was working late, my speed-enhanced sexual desire led me to exercise bad judgment with a co-worker's wife. Fortunately, it did not go too far but far enough so that I was unable to face the music at work. I quit. Ashamed, I could not bring myself to admit to anyone what I had done.

Debbie was aware of the plan I had formulated at work, which if adopted, would increase production at Concord from five boats a week to ten and possibly fifteen. She knew that I had submitted this strategy to Ned, my boss, and Ned had indicated that he did not want Concord that large. He explained he was quite comfortable with producing a mere five boats a week. She knew that I was disappointed that my grandiose plans at becoming a vice president of a major boat manufacturer had collapsed. So, I used my disappointment as my justification for quitting the best job I had ever acquired. Quit the man who had bent over backwards to give me a chance. Quit. I was a good quitter.

Debbie accepted my story and thus began a string of deceptions that drove us deep into the clutches of poverty. Every day I would take Debbie to work and supposedly start a job search. However, the only searching I did was for the ingredients to make a shot of crank. I would spend half the day getting high, and the other half trying to clean the smell from the house so Debbie would not be aware of my duplicity. When questioned about my day's activities, I always had a mendacious tale rehearsed concerning my attempts to locate employment. Debbie would prepare supper, and I would force it down my throat even though the crank I had injected made it taste like cardboard. Yet, my deception required that I eat and so, like it or not, I ate cardboard.

As our financial situation steadily deteriorated, it soon became obvious that we were not going to be able to keep living in our nice home. We started a search for a cheaper place to live. What we could afford and found was a real dump. Still located in Jacksonville, our new home was a very plain and decrepit duplex. I was ashamed to live there.

Was I shamed enough to stop shooting dope and get a job? Not on your life! Was I ashamed enough to crawl deeper in the gutter and rob a drug store? Shame had nothing to do with reality. I embraced the excuse my laziness and deceitfulness provided. Yet my step toward resorting to another crime was a tentative one. I wanted to avoid armed robbery. I told Debbie that I was fed up with the society that would not employ me. I contacted my old friend, Paul Chancey, and had him come to Jacksonville. His arrival insured criminal activity. Paul and I together meant a drug store would be robbed, no doubt about it.

CHAPTER ELEVEN

The Headlights of a Police Car

It is not wise to rush about.
Controlling the breath causes strain
If too much energy is used, exhaustion follows.
This is not the way of Tao.
Whatever is contrary to Tao will not last long.

"Man, what a dump!" exclaimed Paul upon his arrival at the duplex.

"Yeah, love you too, brother," I responded, reaching out to shake my friend's hand.

"Would you like a beer?" Debbie asked him as he took a seat on the couch.

"Sure."

I was sitting at the other end of our couch, which barely fit in the room and Debbie, after delivering the beer to Paul, sat across the room in a chair as we began our war council.

"So, what's on your mind?" questioned Paul, even though he knew where our discussion would lead.

"I want us to go find a drug store we can burglarize," I told him.

Paul was a little amazed that I would consider burglarizing a store since we had graduated to robbery in 1976, but I explained to him that I was not desperate enough to pull an armed robbery. Accepting my reasoning, Paul allowed the discussion to continue and we eventually came to a mutual agreement. Finally, we set about our next goal: to find a worthy candidate.

Within a few hours of travel, we had located our prey, a small town drug store located in a puny shopping center in the metropolis of Vilonia, Arkansas. That same afternoon, after traveling north on Highway 67-167 for about fifteen miles, we arrived in the realm of quaint, rural Arkansas. One feature that made this pharmacy so attractive was its isolation. On both ends of this east to west shopping center were vacant lots and behind it was a pasture. It was situated forty yards from and was lower than the road that fronted it. The area out front was an asphalt parking lot.

There was a gas station and a few other small businesses on the opposite side of the road.

As Paul and I drove past we both realized this was it. We discussed the store as we turned around and drove slowly past again. We both knew that due to the layout and age of the building, we would be able to gain entry into the pharmacy from the roof. The only thing we had to find now was a spot to leave the car while we were committing our crime. We found the solution about fifty yards east of the shopping center, on a small blacktop road that ran south toward the rear of the shopping center. All that remained was to return home, obtain tools and wait for the cover of darkness.

It was after midnight when we returned to Vilonia. The only disquieting aspect to the otherwise dead town was taking place at the gas station, a little east and across the road from the shopping center. Although the station was closed, there was a group of kids gathered around several cars in its parking lot. Most of the car doors were open and car stereos were blasting country music as the kids gathered around drinking beer.

Feeling the effects from the beer we drank earlier, we foolishly decided that we would not let the kids' activity delay our work. We circled back, turned down the side road and drove back to the spot where we would leave the Ford.

Pulling to the side of the road, I turned the headlights off and killed the engine. Paul grabbed our tools, which consisted only of a crowbar and a pair of tinsnips, while I picked up the pillowcase we would use to transport the dope, and we exited the car.

Heading west from the Ford, we immediately had to climb a five-foot high fence that bordered the pasture. Heading deeper into the pasture, we then angled back towards the shopping center. We estimated that we would come out of the pasture behind the pharmacy. It was a short walk, but we had to scale two more fences, one at about the halfway point and the other directly behind the shopping center. Neither of us said a word during this nocturnal trek until we were facing the back wall of the shopping center.

Looking for a way to the roof, Paul spied a group of electrical conduits which emerged through the back wall at shoulder height and ran up over the roof. "Here's our ladder, Bill," pointed Paul. Then without hesitation, he threw the crowbar on the roof and put the tinsnips in his back pocket. He grabbed the conduit and prepared to climb until I stopped him by placing my hand on his shoulder. Paul turned to look at me, and I said, "Your gloves, boy. Don't forget the gloves."

"Oh, yeah … I almost forgot. Thanks!"

We put on our gloves and I followed my partner up the conduit to the roof, a flat hot-tarred expanse with a pea gravel coating.

Our climb did not take us directly above the pharmacy, but a little east of it. We obtained our bearings from the signs at the front of each store that projected higher than the roof. From the roof we could clearly hear the music drifting from the kids' car stereos at the gas station. We retrived the crowbar and walked west across the roof. Suddenly Paul pulled back his right foot and kicked an empty Coke can. As it skidded noisily across the gravel I grabbed Paul, reminding him, "Damn it, man. Stop that! We've got to be sneaky!"

Paul, even in his stupor, quickly realized his foolishness and said, "Right. Sneaky," and held his finger up to his lips.

Without further incident, we located our point of entry directly over the pharmacy. It was a wind turbine, a circulation vent with a diameter of about fifteen inches that protruded three feet through the roof of the drug store.

Paul removed the tinsnips from his back pocket and immediately set to work on the vent. After cutting through the aluminum, he went the entire circumference of the vent, cutting it in two. We laid the top half of the vent on the roof and looked down into the opening.

The hole was too small for me to enter, and Paul volunteered to do the deed. He was to drop in and open the back door for me. I would then help him locate the drugs, and we would exit through the rear door.

Both of us had done this exact same thing before, once even together in the 70's at Park Hill Pharmacy on JFK in North Little Rock.

Paul slowly lowered himself through the vent, stopping to kick a tile section of a drop ceiling out of his way and then extending his arms fully. He let go and dropped into the pharmacy. Suddenly, a cacophony of alarms shattered the night air. It was time to go and go I did! I picked up the crowbar and tinsnips and ran to the edge of the roof. I placed the cutters in my back pocket and, after throwing the crowbar to the ground, grabbed hold of a drainpipe and slid down the back of the pharmacy. I do not know how I managed to make the descent without breaking my neck. I was not even thinking; I was just acting … coming off the roof of that drug store and getting away from that alarm!

Picking up the crowbar, I then leaped over the fence and started running across the pasture towards our getaway car. I was so scared that I forgot about the fence that ran through the middle of the pasture and hit it at a full run. My momentum carried me completely over the fence in a flip, and I ended up flat on my back. I did not even lose my grip on the crowbar; I picked myself up and continued my flight. By the time I reached the edge of the pasture I could no longer hear the alarm so I slowed down, climbed the fence and entered the car. Now that I was at the car, my thoughts turned to Paul. I assumed he would be directly behind me. It should not have taken him much longer to open the back door and get here than it did for me to come off the roof and race for the car.

I alternated between looking into the dark pasture eager to see Paul emerge and down the road behind me, hoping not to see the headlights of a police car.

After what seemed like an eternity but was probably only four or five minutes, I saw Paul emerging from the darkness on the road from behind. I started the car just as soon as I saw him and was primed to drive off as he climbed into the old Ford and closed his door.

"Hang on, Bill," he said.

"Hang on? What for? We need to get the hell out of here!" So saying, I put the car in drive and started down the road, looking for a place to turn around so we could get the hell out of Dodge.

"Bill!" Paul exclaimed, "I took care of the alarm, and there are no cops coming!"

"What about those kids at the gas station? I know they heard the alarm; they'll probably call the cops."

Since we were pulling a burglary, I never expected a quick getaway necessary and had failed to locate a place to turn around, or to have already had the car pointed in the direction we would drive when ready to leave. Therefore, I was forced to waste critical time locating a dirt side road and was in the process of turning around when Paul explained what had transpired.

"Listen, man. The kids didn't hear anything. Stop the car and let me explain."

His calm had just about succeeded in calming my panic. I complied with his request and pulled the Ford to the side of the road. We were almost directly opposite the spot where we had previously parked.

"Ok, tell me."

"When the alarm went off, I immediately went to the back door, but it was locked with a bar running across it and a padlock. Man, I about messed on myself! Then, I ran up front looking for something I could throw through the front window and get out of there. I found a small file cabinet on wheels and pushed it into the front door as hard as I could, man. That door was Plexiglas, and that file cabinet just bounced off! I thought I was trapped! Then, I knocked on the main front window and realized it was glass. About that time, the alarm stopped. Then, I pushed the file cabinet into the window and broke a hole through it big enough for me to get out."

"What about those kids? Didn't they hear the window breaking?"

"I don't think so. I couldn't see them, but I could hear their stereo still blasting and nobody came to check it out. I just ran down the front of the store and through that vacant lot and then down this road. There ain't nothing going on up there. I want to go back and get the dope."

"What!" I exclaimed, "You are crazy!"

"Nah, man. Let's just drive past and see what's going on. If nobody is at the store, why not go back and get the dope?"

This logic defeated my paranoia, at least to a degree, but I let Paul know, in no uncertain terms, that I was not going inside.

"No problem," my bold but sometimes not so bright friend responded.

Sure enough, when we drove past the store, nothing seemed amiss. The kids paid us no attention, and there were no cops. From the road, although you could see the front of the pharmacy, nothing looked out of place. Returning to our parking spot, I gave Paul the pillowcase, and he left.

As I sat there waiting for Paul to return my paranoia started to reemerge and I thought to myself, "Bill, you need to have your head examined!" When a car's headlights wrecked the peace of the hiding darkness, pushing my fear through the roof as I lay down in the seat, I knew it had to be the law, and I was on my way to jail. I started concocting a story about being lost and too tired to continue trying to find my way home. Fortunately, I did not get the opportunity to run this shabby line for the car drove past without even slowing down. As it went by, I sat back up in the seat and watched its tail lights recede into the night.

Finally, after what seemed like hours, I spied Paul's form materializing in the rearview mirror. He seemed in no particular haste, which relieved some of my anxiety, but his hands were empty, which frustrated me. Where was the dope?

As he scrambled into the car, he said, "Let's go."

"Go? Go where? Where's the dope?"

"It's in front of the store. Come on, let's go get it."

"What do you mean, 'It's in front of the store?'" I fired back at him.

"Man," Paul responded, "We've got a bunch of stuff, bunch of guns. Let's go."

I had not even started the car yet, and I was not going to until my crazy, drunken partner clarified himself.

"There were a bunch of guns in that store. I got them. They are in cardboard boxes at the front of the store by the newspaper box. Come on; let's go before someone comes by to fill that box with newspapers."

"What about the dope? Where's the dope?"

Dope was our mission, the whole meaning of this night's escapade. I wanted to know where it was.

"I got it, man. What there was of it anyway," Paul answered in his nonchalant way.

The monster within started to howl with his answer. "Were there any Preluden? Desoxyn?"

"I don't know, don't think so. There wasn't much," he answered. "Come on, let's go. Just pull up front of the store, and we'll load up and go."

I started the car, turned around in the same dirt road, and returned to the drug store. As we turned onto the highway and passed the gas station, we noticed that the kids were gone.

"Paul, did they see you? You think they've left to go get the cops?"

"Nah, they didn't see anything. I heard them drive off about twenty minutes ago. Just pull right in front of the store," Paul directed as I entered the parking lot. "See those paper boxes?" he asked, pointing at a group of yellow and blue newspaper boxes.

I parked the car where he indicated. "Come on, I need a hand. One of these boxes is heavy."

We exited the car, and Paul instructed me, "We'll need the trunk key." I went back to take the keys from the ignition, walked behind the car, and quickly opened its trunk.

Paul was standing beside a huge three feet square box, and, as I approached he squatted down, sticking his fingers under the edge on one side.

"Hurry up, get on the other side."

Facing him, I mirrored his actions, and, as we started to rise, the weight of the box amazed me.

"What the hell is in this thing?" I grunted.

"Guns and dope," Paul explained.

CHAPTER TWELVE

The Potential for Rip-Off is High

What is firmly established cannot be uprooted.
What is firmly grasped cannot slip away.

WRIGHTSVILLE UNIT

"So, were there any Desoxyn or Preluden?" asked Ted.

"No, mostly trash," I answered, looking off into the distance, not at the view through my window at Wrightsville but at the distant past.

"Well, what happened then? Don't leave me hanging," prompted Ted.

"It was one big mess, Ted. The ensuing years brought much robbing, shooting dope, another trip to California, and two parole violations, which netted me sixteen months in prison."

"Did you get arrested for any more drug stores?"

"No, not until 1984. I was picked up a few times, put in a few line ups, but never charged."

"What happened in 1984?" queried Ted.

"Whew, boy! Talk about long and complicated explanations. I better start in 1983."

✗ ✗ ✗

I was released from prison for my second parole violation and returned to Concord Boats to work for Ned Barker. I had made a resolute decision that I was going to get off dope for good.

How could a person who had attempted this feat so many times in the past, all unsuccessfully, even muster the fortitude to make another attempt? Attempts were easy; success was the most elusive animal ever hunted.

I had just spent ten months in prison contemplating my life: thoughts about the family I had lost, the wife I had abused, all the "what could have been and would never be," and the drugs which were the root cause of all that was negative in my existence. The following months provided a very good illustration of what causes the downfall of many drug abusers. We are unable to deal with what I call "kicks in the teeth."

Life is full of kicks in the teeth. Most people find ways to cope with life's brutality. They talk out their pain with a loved one, a pastor, or a shrink. Or they find fulfillment in a hobby or in volunteer work. Drug abusers are not good at dealing with life's knocks. When life's blows hurt drug abusers find solace in their habit. Often the habit takes over their lives and becomes a secret monster. Not knowing how to absorb life's pain—or deflect it one way or another—abusers abuse. In their quest to numb pain, abusers abuse their bodies, their partners, their co-workers. They do not deal with the root cause of their agony.

It was strenuous for me to be back at Concord. The company had changed little in my absence, maintaining a five boat a week production. The factor that was so formidable for me was that I used to supervise the shop and now I was just a flunky. And not just a regular ol' flunky, I was a former production manager who had left under a cloud of smoke. It was a stressful place for me to work, but employment was mandatory when I was released from the joint. Luckily, Ned was kind enough to provide it for me. However, I started looking for another job almost immediately. I wanted to make good on my effort to stay clean and provide a life of normalcy for my wife, something she had not enjoyed since our marriage.

My mother always thought I would make a good salesman, and, since I had no particular calling to speak of, I decided to go with her assessment. I applied and was given a job selling cars for a dealership in Little Rock. I knew absolutely nothing about selling cars but was willing to give it a try. I gave Ned a one-week notice and left Concord for the first time on non-unusual terms.

"Time to go, Babe," I told Debbie through the closed bathroom door.

It was my third day at Little Rock Dodge. I had not sold any cars yet, but I was confident that I would get the hang of it. I looked at my watch again, knowing just how long it would take for me to run Debbie to her job at Systematics where she was a receptionist, and then make it over to University Avenue where I worked.

She was finally ready, and after dropping her off, I went to Little Rock Dodge where my first kick in the teeth awaited me.

"Bill, come to my office, please," said my boss upon my arrival.

I followed him, knowing this did not bode well. I was quickly proven correct.

"Bill, we are going to have to let you go."

"Why?"

"You lied on your application about not being convicted of a felony. We are unable to have you covered by our insurance because of your prior conviction."

"Is there nothing I can do?" I questioned.

"Sorry, Bill."

"Ok, thanks a lot," I responded and then left work feeling the effects of my first kick.

I drove over to the house of Jeff Prince, a guy I had met in prison on my last parole violation. I did not have any plan; I just wanted to talk to someone about my situation, someone who would understand. Jeff is a wiry former hippy with dark, wavy hair and a bustling, pleasing personality. We had become friends in prison and since our releases, had resumed the friendship in the freeworld.

Upon my arrival, I found not only Jeff there but also another fellow ex-con I had met in the joint, Cliff Williams. I did not know this burly ex-biker, who sported arms completely sleeved in prison tattoos, as well as I knew Jeff but liked him enough not to be inhibited by his presence. They were smoking marijuana as I pulled up, and I joined in. Smoking pot was not part of my decision to quit drugs. In my way of thinking, I rationalized that pot was not a drug. I felt pot was not addictive, that it did not damage the body as alcohol did. As we were getting high, I told Jeff and Cliff about what happened at Little Rock Dodge.

"That's messed up," stated Jeff.

"Yeah, especially since I just quit my job at Concord. I have no idea what I'm going to do now."

"Well, you can come with us," said Cliff. "We're going to go to work for this guy in Tennessee sandblasting water tanks."

"Tennessee?" I questioned. "Where in Tennessee?"

"Humboldt," answered Cliff.

"Never heard of it. What's the deal?"

"There is this guy I know who owns a sandblasting company, and he wants me to hire a crew and come to work for him," answered Cliff.

We discussed this proposition throughout the day. The deal was that Cliff's friend wanted him to find two other people who were willing to work on a crew sandblasting water tanks throughout the south. This crew would first go to Humboldt and help get the newly purchased equipment prepared and then hit the road sandblasting tanks that were contracted through his company. The pay for working at the shop in Humboldt was not much but the on site work, the actual sandblasting pay was excellent.

Jeff was planning to go, and Cliff offered to let me be the third member of his crew. It sounded good to me, especially considering my current employment status. It would be a tough sell to Debbie, but I expected she could be persuaded.

Ultimately, it was a hard pill for Debbie to swallow, but she finally agreed to let me give it a shot. The downside of the entire deal was that I would go to Tennessee without her until we got the equipment prepared for sandblasting. I was told that this would only take about two weeks. After that, she could quit her job and travel with me as we went from city to city blasting tanks. The pay was certainly good enough for that.

Things were finally working in my favor; I even obtained permission from my parole officer for this endeavor. Of course, I did not tell him that I was going to go to work with a couple of ex-cons I had met in prison. My parole officer was pretty lax and did not particularly care what I did. I was slated to get off parole in a few months anyway. So, away to Tennessee I went.

I do not believe that I was disillusioned when I set off for Tennessee. Maybe it *was* a questionable decision to leave my wife behind and go off with two ex-cons to another state to work at a type of job I had never done before. I think that at the time, with my fresh efforts to stay clean and with no future that I could discern in Arkansas, it was not an unsound decision.

However, events did not unfold as we had planned or were promised. We ended up being such a good shop crew in Humboldt that our boss did not want to let us go. He offered and then insisted that we remain at the shop working on his equipment. He even hired another crew to take the equipment we were initially promised, equipment we had prepared for sandblasting.

I did not see a future for myself in Arkansas but neither did I see a future as a shop man at a sandblasting company in Humboldt, Tennessee. After six weeks, I caught a ride back to North Little Rock with Jeff and Cliff. Debbie and I had managed to save a few dollars, and we decided to head to Dallas, Texas, to try our luck there. I strongly felt that the best thing I could do to aid my escape from dope would be to get away from Arkansas. I did not want to slip back into the same routine into which I had so often fallen. I wanted to get away from all my dope addict friends and drug stores that I had often visited when in similar situations. So, Debbie and I loaded up our few possessions in our little Vega and drove to Dallas to try and start a new life.

Upon our arrival, we purchased the *Dallas Morning News* and searched the classified ads for a cheap room or apartment we could rent. We quickly found out that an apartment was beyond our meager means and settled on renting a room by the week at the Red Carpet Inn, close to the Love Field airport. Then, we turned our attention to the help wanted section of the classifieds. The ease and success of our search seemed to herald the correctness of our decision to come to Dallas. The next day Debbie found a job as a typist for a temp agency; then I secured employment with a company called Freeman Design and Display, building fiberglass voter registration booths. Both jobs were just temporary, Debbie's lasting an indefinite period, mine lasting six weeks. But they were jobs and acquired on our first full day of searching. We were excited!

With both of us working and now able to supply a reference, we quickly saved up enough money to rent an apartment. We located one in a complex off Northwest Highway, a small one bedroom that was perfect for us.

Debbie and I enjoyed a period of time of living a traditional married life. We were husband and wife with a home and jobs. When the six-week time frame for my job expired, it did not even cause a ripple in our lives. I had done a good job for Freeman, and they gave me a glowing reference that assisted me in obtaining employment with a small manufacturer of custom fiberglass toolboxes for the back of pickup trucks. This job was a long way from our apartment, located northwest

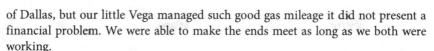

of Dallas, but our little Vega managed such good gas mileage it did not present a financial problem. We were able to make the ends meet as long as we both were working.

A month after starting this job, I dropped Debbie off at work, and as I was driving through a green light at an intersection, a guy ran the red light and broadsided me. I was not injured, but our Vega was finished. The cops arrived and ticketed the guy for running the red light. I was also ticketed for not having any insurance.

I went in a cab that afternoon to pick up my wife from work, and her first words were, "Where is the car?"

"A guy ran a red light this morning on my way to work and totaled it."

My loving wife's second words were concern for my health.

"Nah, I'm ok," I responded.

I told her about calling the insurance company where this guy had coverage and how that tomorrow we could go to this rental agency and pick up a rental for which they would pay until they settled with us on our car. So, things did not look too bad: it was not my fault, the guy had insurance, they were going to rent us a car, and eventually they would pay us for our totaled car and we could replace it. Little did I know that another kick in the teeth was on the horizon.

We picked up the rental car the next day as promised, and life continued on for the next week as it had since we moved to Dallas. I was not planning to make a career at the company that employed me, but it would do for now. The only dark cloud in sight was the fact that Debbie's employment was about to come to an end. The temp agency assured her that they would quickly be able to place her in another position though, so even that cloud was not too dark.

Then came the kick from which I was unable/unwilling to recover. Reflecting upon this event in my life, I see many other options that I could have exercised besides the one I chose. Currently, I do not even see this as a very strong kick, having endured much worse without resorting to my old ways. But at the time, it seemed like a whale of a blow and I snapped. The insurance company gave me a check for two hundred and fifty dollars for my totaled Vega.

"Look at this," I demanded as I arrived home from work and showed Debbie the check I had been given.

"What is this, Bill?" Debbie asked.

"It's the settlement from the insurance company for the Vega."

"Oh, Bill, this won't buy another car. What are we going to do?"

And then I spoke the words I will always regret, "The hell with it! I know how to do this!"

Ah, yes, I knew how to toss in my chips. I was well versed in quitting and giving up. I knew exactly how to deal with this situation.

"I've tried, Debbie. You know damn good and well that I've tried. I'm just not going to be able to get anywhere doing it like this. We will take the money they gave us on the Vega, and I'll buy me a shotgun and rob a drug store so we can get some money to buy us another car."

"Bill, no! Please don't do this!"

"To hell with it, Debbie. They screwed us, and none of this was even our fault. What are we going to do about getting to work? We have to turn this rental in tomorrow."

"I don't know, honey, but we can figure something out. We can take this money and make a down payment on another car."

"We are still making payments on the Vega. No, Debbie. I'll get us some money."

That was it, the decision had been made. Like I had said, "They may as well go ahead and charge me." I knew that at least one pharmacy would be robbed.

WRIGHTSVILLE UNIT

"And that was the beginning of the end, Ted," I explained while sitting on my bed in Wrightsville. "From that decision, I started on a path that did not end until I was arrested in Dallas in 1984 and charged with robberies in Conway, Arkansas and Jackson, Tennessee."

"So you're here for the Conway robbery?" inquired Ted. "What about Tennessee? Will you go to Tennessee when you finish this sentence?"

"No, I beat the charge in Tennessee. If I ever finish this sentence, I'll be done."

"What happened to Debbie?"

"I let her go," I responded. "Fifty years without parole and marriage doesn't go very well together."

CHAPTER THIRTEEN

Fifty Without

If men are not afraid to die
It is of no avail to threaten them with death.

I was sitting in a nine feet by seven feet cell at the Diagnostic unit of the Arkansas Department of Correction in Pine Bluff. The cell had a stainless steel sink/toilet combination and a concrete bed with a crude plastic-covered cotton mattress. I had a fifty-year sentence and a bad attitude.

"Allen, you need to get that bed made up," the guard who was going around doing cell inspections told me.

I just sat there and looked at him.

"Make that bed up right now, or I'll write you a disciplinary," demanded the guard.

"Man, screw you, your disciplinary, and this damn bed!"

What could they do to me, send me to jail? Beat my ass? Kill me? I didn't care. I had just come back from an interview with my counselor and the information he gave had knocked me for a loop.

At our first interview, my counselor told me that because this was my third sentence the law required me to serve three quarters of my fifty-year sentence. That would be thirty-seven and a half years. I was eligible to receive one day of good time for every day of time I completed. This good time would cut that time in half, but I was still looking at doing eighteen and three quarter years before becoming eligible for parole. I argued with him that this was only my second sentence in the ADC and I should only have to do one half of my time before being eligible for parole. This would mean that I would be eligible after twelve and a half years, a difference of six and one quarter years.

I had explained to my counselor that on my first sentence in 1976 I was initially charged with three aggravated robberies. I went to court on the first one in November of 1976 and was sentenced to ten years. Then, I went to court on the other two in March of 1977 and was sentenced to two more ten-year sentences to run concurrently with my first sentence; under the law, this was to be construed as one sentence. He told me that he would check on it. Check on it he did, and the result is what had me in such a blue mood.

"Allen, pursuant to Act 772 passed in March of 1984, anyone convicted of a second or subsequent murder, rape, kidnapping, or aggravated robbery will not be eligible for parole. This means that you will have to serve the entire fifty year sentence, minus your good time."

This was all delivered with a tone and attitude that said, "Argue with me some more and see what it gets you!"

I stood up, ending the interview and was escorted back to my cell where I spent a sleepless night trying to figure out how I was going to do another twenty-four years.

In my head, I had already done two years in different county jails prior to my conviction, and the court would have to give me credit for that time. However, that was time without good time credits and could only be subtracted from the fifty years by itself. That left forty-eight years, and with good time I could cut that to twenty-four years. The year was 1986, and twenty-four years meant that I could get out in 2010. Two thousand ten! That was Buck Rogers' era. I would be an old man, fifty-four years old. I saw no future for me, or rather what future I visualized. I had successfully dug a hole so deep that there was no coming back.

By the time I had completed the medical and psychological testing at Diagnostic and arrived at the Cummins Unit, I had pretty much come to terms with my time. That is not to say that I accepted it or was willing to serve it, but I was able to function and had decided that I should make the best of an adverse situation. There would be no more cussing at guards over silly stuff like the failure to make up my bed. I had not suffered any repercussion over that one incident; the guard probably just figured I was a nut and decided not to write me the threatened disciplinary.

I was medically classified as M3 because of the screws in my left ankle from when I broke it in 1979. This classification meant that I was exempt from the infamous hoe squad. Therefore I was assigned to a catchall job of inside building utility and placed in barracks five on the west hall.

Cummins is an old barracks styled unit that has a long central hallway with open barracks on either side that hold a hundred men in each. The hallway is divided into east and west hall, a division determined by the placement of a hall desk at the halfway point. The hall desk is where the sergeants and shift supervisor, the lieutenant, maintained their post. The east hall is where the hoe squad inmates lived and also where the protective custody barracks, administrative segregation barracks, and the punitive isolation building (east building, "hole") were located. Generally speaking, the east hall is where new arrivals and troublemakers were housed.

If upon arrival you are unlucky enough to be healthy and receive either M1 or M2 medical classification, you are assigned to sixty days fieldwork - hoe squad. You are then placed in an east hall barracks along with ninety-nine other misfits, people who have been busted for disciplinary infractions and placed back on the hoe squad, or other new arrivals who have not completed their hoe squad duty.

It is a harrowing experience for even big, tough guys; for some small, white boys, it was a nightmare come to life. The racial breakdown in the east hall used to be about ten percent white and ninety percent black. I have witnessed instances where one white inmate would be thrown in a barracks where there was only one other white man. Here I use the term "man" loosely; they may be men when they walk through the door, but, ninety percent of the time after their first night, they were punks. Only the strong survive the experience with their dignity intact.

It had been the same experience for me ten years earlier when I arrived at Tucker, serving my first ten-year sentence. I do not remember the racial breakdown being as disproportionate as it was at Cummins, but I clearly remember being viewed as fresh meat upon my arrival. One of the guys who I was with when I first got to Tucker, came to my rack and asked me, "Bill, what are you going to do if someone tries to take your ass tonight?"

My response then reflected my attitude during my entire stay in prison, "I'm going to bust their head!"

"Yeah, but," continued this scared youngster, "what if they wake you up with a razor blade at your throat?"

"Well, I'm not going to say they won't screw me, but they will be screwing a corpse!" I responded. I was then and have always been willing to die to protect my manhood.

Anybody considering a life of crime, including drug use, needs to decide how he will deal with situations like this. There can be no denial that you will be tested, perhaps not sexually, but you will be tested. If you make a life of stealing, raping, robbing, murdering, selling, or abusing drugs, you are going to go down. When you go down, you will be tried. Who looks back out of the mirror at you afterwards will depend on if you had enough heart to defend yourself. If you did not, you are probably not going to be very pleased at the reflection.

However, my testing period was long past and I was not found wanting. My arrival at Cummins was uneventful; I was not a short hair, a term used for first time, new arrivals, dating back to the days when they used to give you a burr haircut on arrival. I had friends at Cummins, and some of them were in barracks five. My first night there was spent getting high on weed and visiting with my friends.

It takes time to understand "doing time" to really know what it is. Janis Joplin said, "Time is just another word for nothing else to lose." Sometimes, I find myself in agreement with her assessment; other times, I do not.

I thought I knew what doing time was. In my past I had completed one two-year stint in prison on a ten-year sentence. I had also served seven months in county jail for the robbery of Lyons Pharmacy, seven months on one parole violation, ten months on another, and two years in county jails prior to my arrival at Cummins. Not quite five and a half years total. Nonetheless, with even that amount of experience, I was little prepared for serving twenty-five years.

On the one hand, I refused to accept that I would be incarcerated that long; on the other, my attitude said in a lot of ways that I had given up on life. The refusal to accept my time was played out by hanging my hat of hope on my appeal. The fact that they had kept me in jail over two years before trying me gave me quite a bit of confidence that I would ultimately win on appeal for a speedy trial denial. I spent months in the prison law library preparing my own appeal to the Arkansas Supreme Court. That kind of effort is not characteristic of someone who has given up on life.

Yet, my activities heralded that I had a total disregard for my own well-being. I was deeply involved in drug trafficking, bootlegging, and gambling at Cummins. All these activities are dangerous in any lifestyle, but within prison, they are tantamount to attempting suicide.

When faced with a fifty year sentence, one thought which comes to mind is, "Kill me. What do I have to live for?" You might also contemplate, "If I'm going to die, let me hit the fence running, lunge over it and fall, dying, outside this prison." It changes you. It affects how you get up and face each new day. But these are the statements and thoughts of those new to having an 'all day' sentence. When I first received this sentence, I could see no light at the end of time's tunnel if my appeal failed. There didn't seem to be any sense in doing 'my time' in accordance with the rules of the ADC. Follow the rules and be in my mid fifties when I got out? Out to what? What was the point?

Most of the early years I spent in prison were in the east hall where the Hoe Squads and other misfits lived. If not in the hole, I was living in barracks nine, composed of inmates who were class two, three or four and usually had some kind of medical restriction which prohibited fieldwork. Inside and outside building utility were catchall jobs for most of us unfit misfits.

My days usually consisted of lying around the barracks getting high, drinking and going out on the yard anytime the door was cracked. I had no contact with the outside world except an occasional letter from my mother and initially some correspondence from my attorney. I supported myself by selling drugs. The drug business in prison was alive and well. The price was exorbitant, but drugs are available for those with the money or hustle to obtain them.

Most inmates have a hustle. The only ones who do not are those who have family on the outside who will support them by sending money in their books and those too sluggish to be resorceful. Hustles are usually associated with job assignments. An inmate working in the kitchen steals food and sells it in the barracks. Even though laundry service is provided free of charge, a laundry worker solicits clients who want their dirty, personal clothes cleaned, insures their return, and provides pressed, starched clothes. Clerks type up appeals and steal office supplies then sell the pens and paper to other inmates.

Not every clerk, laundry worker, or kitchen worker can provide these services;

some because they are not positioned within their job well enough to pull it off and others because of supply and demand. There is only so much supply and only so much demand. So, the rest of us make our hustles in other ways. Some people like me, sold drugs. Some sold their ass. Some preyed on shorthairs or the weak. Some broke into locker boxes or committed robberies. Some just begged.

My hustle was dangerous even though I was not, at this time, into the big deals. When you possess a substance for which people will lie, cheat, steal, or even kill, you are in a dangerous business. Getting a supply of drugs in prison is easy. Every prison has its share of dishonest guards who will sneak them in for a price and visitors can smuggle them in too. Before you can sell drugs in prison, you have to ask yourself one important question, "Will I kill to stop someone from ripping me off?" If you cannot answer that question in the affirmative, you have no business selling drugs in the penitentiary. If just one time you allow someone to steal from you, you are not only out of business, but you will lose all your status and be viewed as less than a man.

Stealing encompasses more than a blatant robbery or burglary. It could be as simple as someone coming up with excuse after excuse as to why they cannot pay their bill. Since most small time drug transactions are on a credit basis, the potential for rip-off is high. I am not trying to present myself to you as someone who was willing to kill over a ten-dollar marijuana debt, but you at least had to present to your customer that that is exactly what you were capable of doing.

One day as I was breaking up a fifty-dollar package of weed and a big, black dude who I had done business with in the past was sitting on the bed next to me. I was dividing the weed into small piles and then wrapping each pile in plastic wrap. This guy asked, "What would you do if I just grabbed all of that and took it?"

I looked him right in the eye and answered, "I would get my shank and stab you in the neck until you were dead." I meant it, and he knew it. He got a dime of weed on credit and promptly paid me the next week.

One incident has remained in my mind over the years concerning the dangers of selling drugs in prison. A black, homosexual inmate who was selling twenty-dollar packages of cocaine in barracks nine in 1987 only had a few papers, but it was enough for a couple of rogues to steal. They strong-armed the homosexual, thinking that he was just another punk, and took his cocaine. They made two mistakes. First, they assumed that this guy's sexual preference equated to him being weak; second, they laid down that night and went to sleep in the same barracks as their victim.

It was about two in the morning, and I was awakened by the noise of metal beds sliding on the concrete floor and screams of pain. I sat up in my bed and saw a man running between the rows of beds from the back of the barracks; another man was chasing him and hit him over the head with a metal pipe. I also saw another smothered in flames running about, crashing into beds, and screaming. An inmate named Ronnie grabbed the blanket off his bed and tackled the burning man, putting out the flames. The other guy, who was getting beaten, managed to gain the front of the barracks, and a guard opened the gate and let him out as other guards rushed in and took the man with the pipe into custody. I will never forget the sights of that night or the smell of burning hair and flesh.

I later learned that the victim of the robbery waited until the two robbers went to sleep and then took a half gallon of paint thinner he had acquired that day and poured it over one guy and lit him on fire. He then rushed to where the other robber slept and started striking him with a metal pipe. Homosexual he may be, but he was never again viewed as weak.

Selling drugs provided me with items that were not issued by the state, such as food from the commissary, stolen food from the kitchen and of course, drugs. Obtaining drugs to sell and use was my largest time-consumer. Many plots and schemes are necessary in order to obtain drugs in prison and is time-consuming. Luckily, time is something I had plenty to spare.

My activities, coupled with my attitude towards authority, time and rules netted me many trips to the hole. For me, the hole was just another place to live. It used to tickle me when officers would threaten me with "locking me up." Lock me up? I was already locked up and the hole held no threat for me.

Years were spent this way. Years that are vague to me, all blending into each other. It was not a life; it was merely an existence. I awoke, got high, did my hustle and went out on the yard. Most evenings were spent getting high, wishing I could get high, or trying to get high. And the years went by.

CHAPTER FOURTEEN

"Hi, yourself,"

Without form there is no desire.
Without desire there is tranquility.

By 1989, I was *lonely*. In June of that year I did something that changed my life for the better. A fellow drugstore robber named Gary suggested that I run an advertisement in a Little Rock free newspaper named, *Spectrum*. This newspaper would run under-thirty-word ads for free.

That very night I composed my ad, borrowed a stamped envelope and mailed it the following day. The ad read:

> *Incarcerated white male seeks white woman for correspondence and possibly visits, age and looks unimportant.*

Many inmates run ads of a similar nature with the sole purpose of obtaining money from gullible freeworlders. I have known guys who ran ads in gay magazines preying upon unsuspecting homosexuals, making promises of coming to live with them upon release if they would help support them while incarcerated. I have heard stories about male inmates pretending to be women and writing steamy letters full of sexual promise if only the freeworlder would help support her so she could afford to feed her cat while in prison. Alternatively, my ad was as sincere as it was blunt. I wanted some contact with the outside world and women.

After several weeks had passed I was sure that my ad had failed its purpose. Then one day in July I heard my name called at mail call. The envelope I was handed was from *Spectrum* and it contained within it another envelope addressed to *Spectrum* and the corresponding code number for my advertisement. Inside this envelope was a three-page handwritten letter. The salutation stated, "Dear Incarcerated White Mal."

The letter was written by a twenty-eight year old, strawberry blond, 4.0 college graduate who speaks, "Spanish, Japanese, some French, German, American Sign Language, etc." I later came to find out the "etc." included Greek. The letter from this highly intelligent and expressive lady named Kathy began:

*I am writing in response to your refreshingly brief and to the point
classified advertisement in Spectrum. I would imagine that you have
either already gotten or will soon get so many responses. I hope so.
All of us have a variety of needs; emotional, intellectual, physical,
Spiritual, etc. So many of us make the mistake of thinking that we
should be able to have all those needs met by a single person. I think
that is sad it limits our experiences. As for my self, I like writing and
receiving letters. I enjoy exchanging ideas. But if you feel it is a waste
of time writing to a woman who offers no possibility of ever becoming
romantically involved, then you better not answer my letter. I am
seeking a correspondent.*

Kathy was wrong on two points:
1. I only received one response to my classified advertisement …
   from her.
2. No chance of romantic involvement. Kathy and I were married
   at a prison wedding service on January 18, 1991.

I quickly responded to Kathy's letter and after a few exchanged correspondences,
I sent her a picture of me and asked for one from her. It is always a scary ordeal
when dealing with the unknown, much like the first meeting on a blind date.
I was hesitant on two accords. The first was my fear that Kathy would be some
three hundred pound ugly hog, thus doing irreparable harm to the image I had
created of her. The second was my appearance and the fear that I would scare her
off. I had been letting my hair grow and the picture that I had taken through illegal
channels showed a thirty-three year old hippie. As things turned out, my fears were
unfounded. Kathy loved my past-shoulder-length hair. The pictures I received
from her were not so favorably received. They were from one of those photo booth
contraptions like you find at malls, where you make silly faces for thirty seconds
and receive a half dozen pictures for your dollar and efforts.

My inspection of the photos revealed a pale white woman with short, blond
hair, which was parted on the side with exceptionally long bangs that hung down in
her face like a shield to hide behind. She appeared to be overweight although not fat,
shy and insecure. If I was not impressed, neither was I put off. We had exchanged a
few letters and I liked her. She was exceptionally bright, wrote lengthy and detailed
letters and sent them often. Besides all that, I had maintained modest expectations
and never clung to the false hope that a beauty queen might respond to a classified
ad from an inmate.

In order for a freeworld person to visit an inmate, a visitation form has to be
completed by the prospective visitor. This form is mailed to the visitation clerk of
the unit where the inmate resides and NCIC (National Crime Information Check)
warrants and criminal history are checked. A search authorization form must also
be signed prior to being approved.

I sent Kathy a visitation form and in September of 1989, she came to visit me for the first time. These meetings were conducted in the visitation room, which is a separate building within the Cummins compound. It is a large room filled with round tables and four colored plastic chairs at each table. Additionally, there is a concession stand run by inmates who are members of the Jaycee organization, and all profits go to that chapter of the organization. The food sold from this stand consisted mostly of packaged sandwiches and soybean burgers, which were then heated in microwaves. Nachos are also a popular staple. As plain as this cuisine is, it was always a treat for me to partake during our visits. It is a far cry above the mundane prison chow.

Visitation for class II, III, and IV inmates at Cummins is on Saturday. Class II-IV inmates are only allowed visits every other week with no visitation on the fifth Saturday of the months that had five Saturdays. Class I inmates visited every Sunday regardless of fifth Sundays. Visitation hours are from noon to four p.m.

At the time of Kathy's first visit, I was Class IV. About eleven a.m. I smoked a joint with a friend of mine named Chuck, combed my hair for about the hundredth time and sat on my locker box to await my visit.

"Chuck, don't you think I ought to put my hair in a ponytail?" I asked, lifting the lid of my locker box and searching for a rubber band to use to tie my hair back.

"Hell no. Didn't she say she liked long hair?"

"Allen, you got a visit," a guard yelled from the barracks door.

I jumped down from my perch. I was as nervous as was humanly possible. With the exception of one visit from my sister, I had not talked to a woman in three years.

"Yes, she did," I answered.

"Then go on, man. Your hair looks fine. Just be yourself; you'll do fine."

"Yeah, you're right. See ya later. Be sure to save me a joint for when I get back."

"Come on, Allen!" the guard yelled.

"I'm coming. Don't get your panties all twisted!" I responded, too nervous to put up with this idiot yelling at me.

"Better watch your mouth, Allen, or you'll be going to the hole instead of for a visit," the guard said as he handed me my visitation pass.

"Ain't no place I haven't been before," I shot back as I was walked down the hall.

The whole visitation process was a bureaucratic ordeal. A visitation pass is a small form on which visitation clerks fill in information concerning the inmate's and visitor's name. I first had to present my pass to a guard working at the doorway that led to the visitation room. He copied the information about me from the pass onto a logbook. When I returned from the visit, he would write the time my visit ended and would know that I did not slip out with the visitors.

Next, I entered into the shakedown area where once again I presented my visitation pass to another guard.

"You got any watches, ring, cross, or any other jewelry?" this guard asked.

"No."

Inmates are not allowed to wear watches or most other jewelry during a visit because it is too easy to wear out something cheap and legal and smuggle in something expensive and illegal. An exception is made for crosses and wedding bands. If I had been wearing either, the guard would have written a description of them on the back of my visitation pass and this would be checked again as I returned. A discrepancy would result in confiscation of my jewelry and a disciplinary would be written.

A cursory pat down revealed no contraband, so the guard handed me my pass and told me to go on. On my return to this room after the visit, the search would be much more complete and intrusive. Much contraband is smuggled from the visitation yard; the two most common are drugs and green money.

With all the preliminaries out of the way, the only thing left for me to do was to walk through the final door and find my visitor. Thankfully, the visitation room was not very full since Kathy had arrived early and it was easy for me to pick her out. She was sitting at a table in the middle of the visitation room, watching the door that I walked through. When she saw me, she stood up. I did not know what I should do when I reached her. Should I try to give her a quick kiss, hug her, or shake her hand? I did not want to do the wrong thing. Fortunately, she solved this quandary for me and instigated a hug herself.

"Hi," I said as I took a seat beside her.

"Hi, yourself," Kathy responded.

"Have any trouble finding the place or getting in?" I asked.

"No, no problems at all. I'm just a bit overwhelmed by all of it. I've never been in a prison before."

I was pleased with this woman sitting before me. I was pleased that she took time out of her life to come and see me. Our visit was productive. It was a feeling out process in which we both became comfortable with each other.

Our relationship continued to grow through our letters and the few visits that were allowed when I was not in the hole. I had always been honest with Kathy, even revealing to her how much time I had to do before getting out. Admittedly, I was optimistic about the possibility of a favorable ruling from the Federal Courts on my case, especially concerning a speedy trial issue. I have no doubt that my optimistic attitude was infectious, and Kathy, being duly infected, believed that a favorable ruling was down the road somewhere, too. Eventually, we fell in love and were married.

There were many ups and downs, not only in those first few months of marriage, but also in all the years that followed. As strange as it may seem, one of the most favorable things to happen in our lives was my obtaining some speed.

Throughout my time in jail and prison, I had craved that "One Shot," the "Monster," the shot that would cross my eyes and sate the monster within me. I had done many shots of dope in prison, but none of them had ever come close to the shot that had led me to risking my life robbing pharmacies. Today would be different; today I would get "The Shot."

An acquaintance of mine, an old convict by the name of Charlie, was scoring crystal methamphetamine. I had been selling enough marijuana that I had accumulated several hundred dollars in green money and had no concern about spending any or all of it to obtain the shot for which I had longed. For eighty dollars, I purchased a gram of crystal from Charlie and returned to my barracks, determined to satisfy the monster that was now howling louder and louder as the inevitable approached.

The threat of AIDS was relatively new to me in 1991, but I had heard enough of it that I was willing to take some precautions to prevent infecting myself. I did not own a syringe, so I borrowed one from an associate drug store robber named Kevin Graham. Kevin is serving a seventy-seven year sentence for robbery and escape. He is one of the most snake-bit people I have ever encountered. Which means, nothing ever goes right for Kevin. The best fortune I ever heard that came his way was when he was allowed to go interstate compact to California, where he had lived before coming to Arkansas.

The syringe I acquired from Kevin was a three-CC barrel with a railroad-spike-size needle on it. After securing the rig, I went in pursuit of some liquid bleach with which I could clean the syringe and needle. I was impatient as hell and the wails and moans produced by the monster in my head, who was not the least bit concerned with infection, almost caused me to end my search and throw caution to the wind. Fortunately, I soon found a barracks porter who had some bleach.

I went to my rack with a cup of bleach and a glass of water, proceeded to fill the syringe with bleach, and squirted it out in my trashcan—an empty five-gallon bucket topped by a board which doubled as a seat or table when required. After several repetitions of this, I rinsed the rig out with water in order to clean the bleach out. There is no doubt in my mind that it was only luck which prevented me from being infected with HIV and not my pitiful attempt to sterilize the rig I was using.

Kevin was sitting on my locker box closely following my every move. I recognized the longing in his eyes, for it had been in my own many times in the past. Kevin was hoping that I might let him have a shot of dope. As I pulled the plastic package from my shirt pocket, he saw just how much I had and asked me, "Bill, can I get a small shot of that?"

Kevin and I were all right, but we sure were not *that* all right. "Sorry, brother, this is all mine."

"Well, how about selling me a shot?" he pursued.

"Kevin, what part of 'all mine' did you not understand? If you want to buy a shot, go talk to Charlie. He's selling. I bought this to scratch a long unscratched itch, and I'm doing the whole damn thing."

"Damn, Bill. You're doing it all? Doing that much will kill you," he exclaimed.

"Nah, ain't going to kill me, but I damn sure bet it crosses my eyes!"

"You got a spoon?" Kevin asked.

I shook my head and he responded by saying. "I've got a good one I stole from the kitchen. Hang on I'll go get it."

I replaced the board on top of my trashcan/chair/table and set the spoon and the glass of water on top of it. Carefully slicing open the heat sealed plastic package with a razor blade, I poured the contents in the spoon. The resulting pile of dope was enough to cause even me to pause, and I sat there for a second considering scooping out a small shot for Kevin. The resulting howls from the monster quickly caused me to abandon such thoughts.

"Bill, you sure you want to do that much in one shot?" Kevin ventured.

"Yep," was my solitary reply? Never having done any of this particular crank, I didn't know what was going to happen when I put water on it. If it was very pure, a small amount of water would cause the whole pile to dissolve quickly. If it was anything like the crap Henry and I used to cook, water could make it grow and turn into thick syrup. Lucky for me, it was about halfway between the two.

I was excited, the monster was excited, even Kevin was excited and he was not doing any of this dope. I strained the liquid through a cigarette filter so that I would not be injecting any of the trash that was left in the spoon and then started to examine my arms for a vein.

I could not find a vein in my hands or arms which I was willing to chance this shot of dope, so I pulled my shoes and socks off and started examining my feet for a likely candidate. My feet were and still are in the same condition as my hands, and there was no way I was going to get this railroad spike of a needle in one of the small veins I found in either place.

My next option was behind my knee on the back of my right leg. I had used this large vein several times but had not tried it since I had abscessed a large shot of Demerol there in 1983. I thought I had located the vein and made a few futile attempts to hit it. This was getting to be more than I could bear; I was so close to getting the shot that would quiet the wails of the monster and I could not find a good vein. I rolled up my left pant leg and inspected behind that knee. Eureka! There was a fat, virgin vein just waiting for its cherry to be popped. The problem and the reason this vein was a virgin was that it is in an awkward spot for a right-handed person to hit. Kevin, realizing my predicament, offered to assist me.

I looked at Kevin long and hard and, finally reaching the only decision I could make, handed him the syringe, turned over on my stomach, and lay on the bed saying, "Don't screw up!"

Kevin pulled off his belt and fed it under my leg and through the buckle, pulling it tight so it would cut off the circulation to my leg and cause the vein to rise. He got it tight and handed the end of it to me and told me to let go when he said.

"Oh yeah, no problem, man. This is a big sucker. This won't take but a second."

Shortly after he made this statement, I felt a jab and knew it would not be long now. Seconds later, Kevin said, "Okay, let go." And then, "I've got it, here goes!"

I did not feel anything. "Are you done?" I asked as I felt Kevin's hands leave my leg. "Yep, got it all and a clean boot."

I started to sit up and then it hit me. Boy, did it hit me! I felt hot all over and my eyes started to lose focus. I never managed to sit up. I just kind of rolled over on my back as this huge wave washed over me. It was exactly what I wanted; the monster was quiet as he fed, the drug rushing through my veins. Kevin was saying something to me; I could barely make out his form standing over me and could not hear his words over the roaring in my ears. Yep, it was exactly what I had wanted, exactly what I had robbed all those pharmacies to obtain. Exactly! And I hated it!

It is difficult to explain; I hardly understand it myself, but I could not stand this feeling. I was wishing that I were straight, regretting that I done this shot. What coherent thoughts my mind could still form centered on the idea that I would never do this again. To this day, over ten years hence, I have kept this promise to myself. I tell people who ask me how I was able to just quit drugs, "It was almost like magic. It was like a fairy godmother waved her magic wand over my head and said, 'From this day forth, you will never desire drugs again.'"

From that day in 1991, the monster has not raised its ugly head, and I have heard neither whine nor whimper from it. The desire has been totally excised. It was the best thing that had ever happened to me and although I am grateful, I just wish I had some recipe that I could share with others who really wish to get the monsters off their backs.

Bill Allen, 2007

*Bill Allen in the
Cummins Prison, 1986*

*Bill Allen,
Cummins Unit, 1991*

*Bill and Kathy at
Cummins Prison,
1988*

*Bill and Kathy at
the Wrightsville
Unit, 1993*

CHAPTER FIFTEEN

Five New Words

*A journey of a thousand miles
begins with a single step.*

Now that I had stopped shooting dope, what was I supposed to do? I did not have the slightest idea of where to go from here. I had stopped getting disciplinaries and had secured a job working for Captain Lang in staff dining. Simply getting this job was a big step for me. For one thing, I felt like I was crossing the line, working for the officers. As a convict, working for "the man" seemed to be a conflict of interest. Had it not been for a friend of mine, someone I respected, taking the same path about a year previously, I would not have taken the position. Ronnie Branch had worked in staff dining for about nine months before he left to go to a county jail in southern Arkansas as part of the Act 309 program. I convinced myself that if Ronnie could hold down such a job and never be labeled in the wrong light then so could Bill Allen. As far as I know, I was correct.

The new job provided me with a barracks change, a very advantageous move to barracks one, the pods. The pods are all single man rooms, complete with air conditioning, a writing counter, and a personal sink. There was even a door to which I had the only key. To anyone who had lived for years crowded in open barracks, a move to the pods was quite an event.

I had succeeded in improving my situation, in changing my living status, but I had not done anything that could be termed improving myself other than quitting drugs. So I took advantage of the privacy of my new room and started spending some time thinking about my life. I had screwed up big time! The year was 1991, and I was still looking at over twenty years until my release date. Of course, I had not accepted that I would have to remain in prison that long. However, that was what my time card said, and, unless something happened, that was my sentence. I sat down one night with a pen and paper and started listing my good and bad qualities. Reviewing what I had written, I decided I would start working on enhancing my good qualities while reducing the bad. One of the favorable qualities I had listed was my intelligence, and I decided to capitalize on that one first.

Christmas of 1991 was approaching, and Kathy asked me what I wanted. I asked her to get me a dictionary and used it to start reviewing words that were unfamiliar to me. Each week, I would study five new words, send the list I was studying to Kathy, and on visit she would test me. Five words may not seem like much, but it was a start; I had to start somewhere. I still have this dictionary, and, every time I spot a word in it that has a small dot beside it, it reminds me of my very first step.

One day during this time, I saw a memo on the barracks bulletin board advertising PMA (Positive Mental Attitude) class. I decided that this could be something that would help me, and I signed up for it. As it turned out, this was not only a correct decision, but also a monumental one which has had a favorable impact on my life ever since.

The classes were every Wednesday night in the unit's school building. Also being held in the same buildings were college classes that were available for not only the Cummins unit but also a neighboring unit, Varner. One evening as the people attending the PMA class were waiting in a fenced in area front of the blood bank, a now discontinued inmate plasma center, the inmates from Varner who were attending the college classes arrived. I was leaning against a fence waiting for a guard to unlock the gate when I recognized one of the inmates, Bobby Futch, the guy who drove for me for the Lyons robbery and who testified against me at the ensuing trial.

He did not see me until I was standing right in front of him. All the emotions I had stored up over the years came bursting forth, and the only thing that stopped me from attacking him was the fact that I was attempting to change. Regardless, my attempts to change did not stop me from lambasting him verbally and, had he taken exception to that, I would have done what I had to do.

"Well, well, well, if it's not that snitching punk, Bobby Futch! How are you doing, Bobby?"

"Come on, Bill. Please don't start that," replied Bobby.

I ignored his plea and turned to all those gathered within the fences. "Hey, ya'll. This is a snitching punk. In 1980, I watched him sit up on the witness stand and testify against me for a drug store robbery."

"Bill, you know I just did what your lawyer told me to do. I helped you beat that charge."

"Helped me beat it? You lying ass! If it hadn't been for your snitching, I never would have been arrested." My rage was pouring out, and I was close to losing what little control I had mustered.

I actually wanted Bobby to try me. I had said things to him that a man, be he free or inmate, would not have allowed. But Bobby is a coward. He was a coward when the police arrested him, he was a coward at court, and he was still a coward as he faced me at Cummins. Fortunately, the guard arrived and unlocked the gate, and we were ushered to our respective classes.

The next week as I waited for count to clear so we could go to our PMA class, the entire PMA group was in the hallway between barracks one and two. Down the hall came the group from Varner, and they mingled among us from Cummins. I was sitting down on one side of the hallway when Bobby and I saw each other; he stopped and sat down on the opposite side of the hall. I looked at him for a full five minutes and then stood up and approached him. As he saw me coming towards him, Bobby stood to face me, fear and resignation written on his face. When I was standing right in front of him, I looked long and hard in his eyes. Finally, not being able to weather my intense stare, Bobby asked, "What's up, Bill?"

"Bobby, for eleven years I have hated you and could think of nothing else but if the opportunity ever arose, I would kill you. I am tired of living with this hate, and I am going to forgive you and let all of that past hate and anger go." So saying, I stuck out my hand for him to shake.

Bobby initially flinched as my arm extended, ready for me to throw a punch. Then, he realized that I was serious and relief overwhelmed him and his eyes threatened to spill tears. He clasped my hand as hard as a drowning man would grasp a lifeline.

"Bill, I don't know what to say. Man, I'm sorry."

"Forget it, I have made many mistakes in my life that I would like to be forgiven for."

With that, I turned and walked away a different person. I felt high; a sense of well-being came over me as years of hatred were washed away. It must be akin to what a new Christian feels when he confesses his sins and is born again.

I genuinely felt like I had taken the first step. Yet, first steps must be followed by a second, then a third if one is to make progress. I had no idea of how I was going to accomplish so much but had an idea of where I wanted to go. I wanted to become a person who could not only get out of prison but also stay out.

Kathy was a very good influence on me. For the first time in my life, I took into account somebody's love for me. It mattered that she loved me. It mattered what she thought of me. It mattered the way my accomplishments or failures impacted her life. I liked the way it made me feel when I told her that I was done shooting drugs, when I told her the story about Bobby and my forgiveness of him. Even simple things such as trying to improve my vocabulary and spelling pleased her, and her pleasure in turn made me feel good. This was a new experience for me.

A year followed in which I maintained class and my job in staff dining. During this time, there were many occasions when I would tell myself, "Ok, I have learned what I needed to learn; I am ready to go home." Then, something else would happen which would prove to me that I was in fact not ready for release. However, I would take these instances as lessons and would be grateful that I was able to learn the lesson prior to my release.

Even with the big change in attitude I had undergone, I had not given up smoking weed. I mean, come on, weed? What does weed hurt? I had quit shooting dope, was not that enough? Was it not speed that got me into prison? Weed never hurt anything.

Wrong. If the penalty for smoking marijuana exceeded what one was willing to pay, then smoking pot could hurt. There are many other lessons I subsequently learned about marijuana, but they are not germane to my story at this point. The penalty is, however.

It is Christmas eve 1993, and I am in my room with a friend named Raymond, a big, good natured guy with whom I got along well. We were doing our part to celebrate Christmas by getting high on some weed.

"Don't bogart that joint, my friend," I told Raymond, as he had a tendency to hang on to the joint for increasingly long periods.

He took another toke as I noticed a shadow approaching the door. "Look out!" I warned Raymond.

He had the smoking joint up to his lips just as a guard peered through my window. Raymond quickly snatched the joint from his lips. That probably generated more suspicion than if he had slowly moved it and pretended that he was smoking a cigarette. However, the ultimate error was mine; I was supposed to be watching while he smoked. The guard did not pause, knock on the door, or anything, he simply went on.

Raymond immediately extinguished the joint and asked me, "Did he see it?"

"I don't know, man. But we better get ready."

"I'm going to my house; I'll be back later," Raymond said as he left my room.

We did not have more weed, so I was not worried about a shakedown; it was a urinalysis that concerned me. Urinalysis testing for drug use is one of the things that really amazed me when I first came down on this sentence. In the past, it made little difference if a cop had seen us smoking a joint as long as we could beat a shakedown. But the "Drug Wars" had even had their effect in prison and the administration and GI Joe cops in prison loved it. It was now payback time for all those slick convicts that had been beating them at the drug game for so many years.

Drinking water is the only sure fire way to beat a urinalysis. You had to drink a lot of water to accomplish this, and when I say "a lot," I mean a lot! Additionally, time was a factor because it would take awhile for this water to run through your system to flush it out. Of course, the powers that be have gotten wise to that now and usually give very little warning prior to testing; plus, if the laboratory to which they send the test for analysis reports that your test had too much water, they test you again.

Worried that they would be calling my name soon, I immediately started drinking water, lots of water. I grabbed my soap, shampoo, and towel and headed for the shower, where I drank some more water. My big concern was getting some time so I could flush my system out.

Sure enough, about five minutes after I began showering, Raymond came by and told me the police were calling for us to go to the hall desk. "Ok, tell them I am in the shower and will be there in a little bit."

About five minutes after that, the same guard who obviously reported us came to the bathroom and told me, "Allen, they want you at the hall desk."

"Ok, I'll be there directly," I replied.

All the while I was drinking as much water as I could stand. This is an awful experience; it has you all bloated and causes headaches. About another five minutes went by before the guard came up again and said, "Allen, come on. They want you at the hall desk."

I turned the water off and said, "Damn it. What's the hurry?" and started drying off as the guard left.

I had stalled as long as I could. A few minutes later, four police came up and told me to come on; I was going to the hall desk right then. They escorted me to my room, stood around as I dressed, and escorted me to the hall desk. Once I arrived, the sergeant on duty told me to go stand against the wall directly in front of the major's office. Raymond was standing there as I arrived.

"Have they tested you?" I questioned him.

"No, they have been waiting on you, I think. The captain is getting hot."

"Have they questioned you?" I asked.

"No."

The major's office door opened and out came Captain Cash. "There you are, Allen. Which one of you is ready to piss first?"

Raymond and I looked at each other, and Raymond said, "I'll go first."

He and the captain went into the major's office and shut the door, leaving me to stand on the wall. I was racking my brain trying to figure out what to do. Everything I was working for was in jeopardy. I had managed to go since June of 1990 without a disciplinary, and that two and a half years of clean record was about to be literally pissed away.

It was only a few minutes before Raymond, followed by the captain, came out of the office and as Raymond walked off, returning to the barracks, the captain asked me, "You ready, Allen?"

Despite my efforts, I was served a disciplinary for use of drugs on January 9, 1993. Fortunately, this was during a brief period of time in which the administration was being lenient on failed urinalyses. In the past, you stayed in administrative segregation until you went to disciplinary court. Then, if you were found guilty in disciplinary court, you were busted to class IV, lost up to a year of good time, and sentenced to thirty days punitive isolation. For some reason, the administration was exercising less stringency at this time and only busting those who failed urinalyses two steps in class. Since I was class I, I was reduced to class III.

This was catastrophic for me. I had been living in barracks one with my own room for a year and a half. I was able to go from one end of the prison to the other without question. I had been working in a good job. My entire life had changed since my early days of not caring. Kathy was a major factor in my life change. She had given me reason to want to live. She had given me hope for a better future. Now, I was being returned to barracks nine on the east hall and reassigned to inside building utility. Back into an open barracks, back into a job that held no status. Back was the key word here; I had been moving forward, and this backward movement opened my eyes. I had quit using drugs but had hung on to marijuana, thinking that there was nothing wrong with it. This was the first time that I had ever considered that there might be. Namely, if getting caught smoking pot causes you to suffer consequences beyond what you are willing to pay, it is wrong for you to smoke it.

I had been busted for smoking or possessing pot a half dozen times before this, but even though the penalty was harsher at those times, it did not bother me. This bust bothered me greatly, and I was learning a lesson and telling myself once again, "I am glad I didn't get out before I learned this lesson!"

CHAPTER SIXTEEN

The Lowest Rung on The Kitchen Ladder

See simplicity in the complicated,
Achieve greatness in little things.

I quit smoking pot. Unfortunately, this was not the magical cure I had undergone with quitting dope. This was a struggle from the first day, every day, and today. The first test came quickly. As soon as I moved into barracks nine, a friend approached me and told me when I got settled in we would get high. I declined, explaining that I was going to quit smoking pot.

"Hell," my friend responded, "the time to quit was before you got busted, not after."

"Yeah, but another bust is just down the road, and I want no part of it," I responded.

I managed to survive my time on the east hall without getting high or into any other trouble, and in sixty days I was given class II, reassigned to the kitchen, and moved to the west hall and barracks five.

Captain Lang, the food management supervisor, always liked me, and he pulled the necessary strings to get me reassigned to him. My first job was as a cart-man, preparing the food on carts for adminseg and punitive isolation. Adminseg is prison slang for Administrative Segregation, which—like punitive isolation—is a section where troublesome inmates are housed. I would then push the carts down the hall for the officers to feed the inmates who were locked up. Once they were all fed and the trays picked up, I would go retrieve the carts and return them to the kitchen. It was not a very prestigious or rewarding job, but I knew that I had to work my way back up; I had to start somewhere.

About two weeks later, Captain Lang asked me if I wanted to work in the storeroom. This was a step up, and I gladly accepted, knowing that once I was class I again he would put me back in my old job in staff dining. Sure enough, when I was eligible for class I, the captain put me up for classification for both class I and a job change to staff dining. Since I had a two and a half-year track record prior to this last bust and because I had done a good job in staff dining previously, the classification committee approved the class and job. I was allowed to return to barracks one and a private room.

In a ninety-day period, I had come full circle. But was I worse or better off than before? One of my main goals was to obtain IB trustee status, and, in order for me to do that, one classification officer had told me, "Bring me five years as class IC." I had managed to do half of that amount of time before I got busted; so, in that regard, I was worse off. I had blown a two and a half-year track record. On the other hand, I was clean: my system was clean, my behavior was clean, my room was free of contraband. I was successful, to this point, in staying off weed, and that was the single biggest risk I had been taking for a couple of years.

It was by no means the only risk I had been taking because it was not only smoking it that was so dangerous; it was also obtaining it so that the habit could be supported. I had quit the small time hustle of selling dimes of pot because that was front line dealing, and everybody knew your business, including the folks. For the past couple of years, I had been involved in much bigger things, things that few people knew about and brought much greater financial rewards. The details of this activity are not relevant to this tale; the fact that I was no longer involved in them is. I was now involved in no activity that would cause me to get busted again.

One day as I was working in staff dining, the new classification officer, Mr. Taylor, came in, and, as I served him his meal, I asked him if I could come to his office and speak with him for a minute whenever he had time. Upon completion of his meal, he stood up, walked toward the door, and said, "Come on, Allen."

I followed him to his office, and we entered. Mr. Taylor sat at his desk and asked me, "What's on your mind, Allen?"

"Mr. Taylor, what do I have to do to get class IB?"

He just sat there, looked at me for a moment, and then asked, "How much time do you have left, Allen?"

"Nineteen years."

"What you need is a transfer, Allen. How do you get along with Major Benedict?"

Major Benedict used to be the classification officer at Cummins and had been promoted to building major at the Wrightsville unit. It was Mr. Benedict who I had previously asked the same question I was now putting before Mr. Taylor and the one who told me to bring him five years at class IC. We knew each other well, and I had always liked and gotten along with him.

"I get along fine with Mr. Benedict," I responded.

"What I think I will do is transfer you to Wrightsville. There you will have a clean start and possibly get your IB there."

"Thank you, Mr. Taylor."

For the most part, I was excited about my transfer to Wrightsville, but I still had some reservations about the move. I have known people who had been transferred there and who immediately set to work to get transferred back to Cummins. Cummins was where it was at: drugs, easy movement, and obscurity. Compared with some of the smaller units, Wrightsville included, Cummins was wide open.

However, it was that kind of life I wanted to escape. I needed a new environment in order to continue to grow. Plus, I could leave the old Bill and most of his record behind. Of course, my institutional jacket went with me to Wrightsville, and all my past disciplinaries were there for anybody within the administration to see. Yet, here was an opportunity for me to make fresh first impressions, and perhaps I could get IB trustee status there.

It was quite an experience even riding in the van to Wrightsville. I had not been outside the Cummins unit but once in the seven years I had been there and riding in a motor vehicle was a trip. The first curve in the road we approached I just knew we were going to wreck. There is no way a vehicle, much less a fifteen-passenger van, could make that turn at that speed and remain on the road. The fact that we were probably only doing forty-five miles per hour escaped me. It felt at least like we were traveling one hundred miles per hour. At the first stop sign we approached, it was all I could do to keep from throwing myself on the floor preparing for the crash. We approached it so fast; I knew we would never stop. Sure enough, we did and it was not even a hard felt skidding or sliding stop. We leisurely pulled up to the stop sign and stopped with hardly any noticeable G-forces.

Once I got used to the speed of travel, I started looking through the bars on the van's windows at the outside world. It looked pretty much the same. Many of the cars I saw I could not recognize the make or model but, all in all, it looked like the same world.

I started looking at the people who drove the cars we passed and thought, "That guy there is free. If he wants to, he can turn left on that road up there. He could turn completely around and go home if he wanted to." It made me feel funny inside to have thoughts like this, to realize there were people who could do what they wanted. What an amazing concept!

Upon our arrival at Wrightsville, the two other transfers and I were unloaded at the sally port. I had all my property in one cardboard box and set it beside a fence as directed by the officer. He then ushered us through a metal detector and told us to have a seat on a bench in a little room that comprised the sally port office.

Soon a large man entered the office, followed by an inmate carrying a blue milk crate with our three jackets inside it. The man sat in a chair behind the desk while the inmate set the crate of jackets on the floor beside the chair.

"My name is Mr. Step. I'm the classification officer here at Wrightsville. I'm going to assign each of you a job. I'll talk to you one at a time. Once you have been assigned, you will take your property and go to the laundry to get bedding and a locker box. The laundry is just down this road on your right." Then he vaguely waved his arm in the direction the road.

"Allen, you stay in here, you other two go wait outside. When Allen leaves,

Johnson, you come in. Bye," he said, waving his arm again, dismissing the other two.

Mr. Step reached down and finding my jacket, pulled it from the milk crate. As he opened it, I stood up and approached the desk, standing in front of it, lightly clasping my hands behind my back, trying to present a totally non-threatening, adaptive attitude, the type of posture the powers that be like for us inmates to adopt.

"Allen, I see you have kitchen experience. I also see you like to smoke dope. Report to Captain Kenny in the kitchen tomorrow." I was dismissed.

"Yes, sir," I responded and following his first set of instructions, exited the office, found my property and left the sally port for the laundry.

An inmate opened the gate for me to leave the sally port and I started walking down a paved road looking for the laundry. Wrightsville was completely different from Cummins. Everything at Cummins is essentially contained in one big building; Wrightsville reminded me of a small college campus. The barracks were in individual buildings that looked like houses. Wrightsville is comprised of thirteen barracks, a laundry, kitchen, gym, maintenance building, school building, and an industrial complex, all within a single security fence surrounding the compound.

I eventually found my way to the laundry and was from there directed to the security building where I would be assigned a barracks. I entered the front door and presented myself to an officer working the desk who told me to stand on the wall and they would be with me in a minute. I set my newly acquired locker box, which replaced the cardboard box and now contained all my property, on the floor and stood against the wall as directed.

"Are you Allen?" an inmate I did not recognize asked me.

"Yes."

"Bill Allen, from Cummins?"

"That's me."

"Ok, Allen. Snuffy told me to tell you that he's got you. We are going to put you in barracks eight," this unknown inmate informed me before he left.

Cool. A guy I had known at Cummins, who was the security clerk at Wrightsville and responsible for assigning beds and barracks was looking out for me. That is the way it is supposed to work, convicts looking out for other convicts.

As I waited, the other two transfers arrived and were also told to stand on the wall. A few minutes after the last arrival, Snuffy Smith came into the room and approached me.

"Bill Allen, how ya doing, brother?"

"I guess I'm doing ok, Snuffy. I don't really know the jury is still out; I just got here. Good to see you, man."

"This place is ok, Bill. I think you'll like it here. Listen, I got you a rack in barracks eight; that is the clerk's barracks. There are a few kitchen workers in there, so I can justify putting you in there to the major; we shouldn't have any problem. You know Benedict, don't you?"

"Yeah, know him pretty well," I answered.

"Good, like I said there shouldn't be any problem. I'll see you this evening when I get off work." He stuck out his hand and we shook.

"Ok, Snuffy. Thanks for looking out for me."

As Snuffy turned to leave, he gave the officer a piece of paper which had our barracks and bed assignments.

"Johnson," the officer said. "You go to 5-13. Dickerson, 5-42. Allen, 8-21."

These were our barracks and bed assignments; I was going to barracks eight, bed twenty-one. I picked up my locker box, looked at the officer, and asked, "Where is eight?"

"Directly behind this building and a little to the right," he instructed.

I left security and found barracks eight and ultimately my bed. I had noticed several buildings on the compound that looked like barracks eight and the best way to describe its outward appearance is like a medium size, red brick house you would see in many suburbs across America. The interior was quite different from a regular house. Close to the front door, there is an office in which the security officer works. There is a day room with a TV at each end and benches on which to sit for viewing programs. On each end of the barracks, there is a large room filled with beds and locker boxes. In each of these two large rooms, twenty-five inmates live. There are also four smaller rooms, two of which house eight inmates and the other two, six. These semi-private rooms were the coveted spots in each barracks. My bed was in the large room at the south end of the barracks. There were quite a few people that I recognized living in the barracks with me, none of whom I would call friends. I spent the remainder of the afternoon visiting with a few people and getting the low down on the unit. Eventually, I located someone who also worked in the kitchen as a clerk, and he told me I would not be on the roster in the kitchen for a couple of days and suggested that I go see Captain Kenny in the morning.

When Snuffy came in that evening, he came to my rack and told me to come with him. I followed him into one of the semi-private rooms that he shared with two other inmates. I immediately recognized that this was where I wanted to be.

"What does it take to get into one of these rooms?" I asked Snuffy as I took a seat on his locker box and he sat on his rack.

"Well first of all, obviously, there has to be an opening; then the Major reserves these for clerks. However, there are a couple of officers' mess workers living in one of the other ones. Step assigned you to the kitchen, didn't he?"

"Yeah. What do you think the chances are that I can work in staff dining?" I did not think this was beyond the realm of possibility, seeing how I had a few years of experience working officers' mess and that was my last job assignment.

"No problem, if they have an opening, but you'll probably have to work your way up in the kitchen, first. I'll talk to Captain Kenny and put in a good word for you."

Snuffy also filled me in on more of the low down about my new home and asked if I had called anyone to let them know that I was here.

"Call? How do you do that?" I asked. I had not used a telephone in many years and was amazed at the prospect.

"Just go tell the officer that you just got here today and you want to call your family and let them know you are here. It has to be an immediate family member: wife, parents, brother, or sister."

I had no idea what Kathy's phone number was, I had never called her. So I decided to call my mother. She and I had been writing on a regular basis for a couple of years and I was certain that she would accept a collect call.

Thinking about this brought up a memory of years past. I was eighteen years old and on the run from the Sherwood Police Department. I had violated probation for a possession of marijuana with intent to sell charge, and my probation officer asked me if I wanted to join the service for two years or go to the penitentiary for one. I had told him to process the paper work for me to join the service and I would go pack.

Pack I did. I packed my Boy Scout backpack and hit the highway. I had been gone for about six months and was temporarily living in a little town in Colorado. I decided to give my parents a call.

"Hello," my mother answered the phone.

"Collect call for anyone from Bill," the operator told her.

I could hear the conversation and heard my mother ask my father, "Jake, do you want to accept a collect call from Bill?"

"Bill who?" I could hear my father ask.

"Your son, Bill," my mom responded.

"I don't have a son named Bill," my hardhearted father responded.

"No, operator. We will not accept," my mother said softly.

I did not expect that to happen with this call even though my father and I were not getting along. I had written him several times to no avail, but I did not think he would refuse my call.

Fortunately, he did not answer, and I explained to my mother about my transfer, asked her if she would find Kathy's phone number, give her a call, and let her know where I was. It was nice talking to my mother as I had not seen or talked to her since my trial in Tennessee, seven years ago. She even asked me to send her a visitation form, since I was so close to Little Rock now, and she would come see me. I got off the phone feeling good and went to bed that night more optimistic than I had been in years. Designer: I am not able to omit this rule. Please omit it and use normal pgh spacing here, no more.

I went to the kitchen the following morning and found Captain Kenny in the office. He promptly assigned me to the morning shift washing pots and pans. I would have to work my way up, pots and pans being the lowest rung on the kitchen ladder. However, I felt equal to the task.

CHAPTER SEVENTEEN

Helping Myself by Helping the Blind

Without form there is no desire.
Without desire there is tranquility.

By the time Sunday arrived and Kathy came to see me, I had decided that Wrightsville was not the place for me and wanted to leave. Standing over a steaming sink scrubbing huge pots and pans did not seem like the ideal way of doing time. However, that was not the only issue. For years I had become accustomed to having the opportunity to go out on the yard during the day and run. At this unit, yard call was not until after shift change, six thirty p.m. and the yard was awful. Cummins has a track around its yard, which measured four tenths of a mile. The track around Wrightsville's yard was only about two tenths of a mile, and it was not even close to level. Besides being too small for the long distance running I enjoyed, the Wrightsville yeard was too tiny to accommodate the four hundred inmates who would appear at yard call. Running around it involved numerous near misses and sometimes collisions with inmates who walked its circumference as I ran. Then there was the softball field, the outer edge of it formulating the track, there were times that errant throws and hits actually injured runners and walkers alike. Additionally, yard call here was only from daylight savings time in the spring till daylight savings time in the fall, which would totally ruin my workout schedule. I had worked too hard to get where I was to let this place screw it all up for me. Yes, I hated it. Hated the crowded conditions, the limited schedule, and probably just because it was not Cummins, the place I was used to.

"I'm ready to go back to Cummins," I advised Kathy after we sat down to eat our soybean burgers and nachos.

"Why, Bill?"

I proceeded to tell her the aforementioned reasons, leaving out one of the biggest ones because I knew it was hard to explain and would not generate much sympathy from my wife.

This reason was that convicts, more so than most people, resent change. We get used to doing our time in certain ways and do not like changes thrust upon us. Falling into patterns year after year makes a person become institutionalized. I would not want the characterization of being institutionalized placed on me at this point, but I had found ways to fill my days and had become comfortable with doing my time in that manner. I was out of my element at Wrightsville and was extremely uncomfortable.

"Bill, I sure wish you would reconsider. You know that you being here is much easier on me than having you all the way down there at Cummins. It took me all of ten minutes to drive here today, opposed to the two hours it takes to drive to Cummins. Please, give it some time and see if you don't like it here better."

What could I say to refute that argument without making me seem like a real heel? Kathy had never complained about the long drive to visit me at Cummins, never complained about all the hassles that visitation at a prison involves. This would be the first time I had a genuine opportunity to do something for her. After all she had done for me, I could not do anything but oblige.

"How much time?" I asked.

"Give it a year, Bill. If you still want to go back to Cummins after a year, I'll never voice any objection."

"Ok, I'll do that. Kathy, I do appreciate all you do for me, the visits, the money, everything."

"I know you do, sweetie."

✗ ✗ ✗

Fortunately, my stay in pots and pans was brief. As new people came to work in the kitchen, they would replace those working pots and pans. After one such substitution, my supervisor told me that he wanted me to work on the serving line.

"Fine, I'll work on your line, but the first time somebody comes through here and calls me a punk or a bitch, I am coming over that line and kick their ass."

"Oh, no, we can't have that. I'll tell you what, Allen. You work in the dish room."

This was a much better place for me. I have heard too many people going through the chow line talking bad to the servers, and I knew that I would never make it there.

I worked in the dish room for about thirty days while I attempted to find a comfortable routine. I would go to work at 4:00 a.m. and get off at 11:00 a.m. This left a lot of free time on my hands, which I filled with reading and writing Kathy. I also, even though I hated the limited hours, participated in yard call and continued running laps. Several times I let Captain Lang know that I had experience in staff dining and that I would like to work there when he had an opening. I never obtained a firm commitment from him; he just said he "would look at me." I hate that response, a favorite of the powers that be.

My mother came to see me soon after my arrival at Wrightsville. This was a very emotional event for me; it had been seven years since I had seen her. The last time was at my trial in Tennessee. That first visit with my mother, who was now sixty-three years old, brought to light my mortality and how short our lives are here on earth. However healthy she was, my mom had aged, and that aging was blatantly apparent to me since my mental image of her did not align with who was in front of me. .

I came face to face with the reality that my mother may very well die before I ever get out of here. Realizing this possibility made me extremely uncomfortable and added another reason for me to pursue trustee status. At least with IB, I could possibly get a furlough and be able to spend some time with her before she died.

✗ ✗ ✗

Firm commitment or no, when an opening came up, the Captain did put me in staff dining. The timing was perfect because an opening was coming in Snuffy's room too, and within a week of my job change, I moved into the semi-private room with him.

Captain Kenny asked me to give him six months working in the kitchen before allowing a job change. Working staff dining was not bad; it did not carry the status or perks that it did at Cummins, but it was better than most positions. Being the one to serve the guards their food allowed me to become a person who's favor they sought. I was the food giver, if something decent was served, it was at my discretion to be able to give more than their issue. This allowed me some extra leeway when I wanted to do something that was technically against the rules. The guards would allow me to go places, visiting other barracks for example, that most could not. It also allowed me to build up a reserve of uncashed favors in case some disaster came my way. Say for example, a guard loves fried chicken and I serve him extra. This goes on for a couple of months and I never ask him for anything, then one day I find myself in trouble. I can go to the guard whom I had been giving extra fried chicken and seek his help in getting me out of a jam. So working in this new job was ok, however, it would never gain me trustee IB status. Kathy asked me to give her one year at Wrightsville; I gave her six. Captain Kenny asked for six months; I gave him ten. During those ten months, I had become accustomed to Wrightsville and was no longer eager to leave. In prison, just like anywhere else, you develop a routine, you get comfortable. I had adjusted to Wrightsville. I knew the guards, convicts and inmates plus the administrative individuals who all make a prison function. I had even made a few friends. I knew the ins and outs of the place and realized that I could be more here than just another screw up. I was the guy in Staff Dining that the Major could pull to the side and whisper to me, "Allen, I hear they are having cake with icing today. You know I like cake with icing." When it rained, I knew the shortest path where the least drops would hit me. When it was hot, I knew the coolest places to go. I knew my way around … I was comfortable.

I had also spent time checking out the job opportunities which the unit provided. I found one place that interested me more than any other: the Wrightsville Braille project. I did not know anything about Braille except it was a raised letter writing that enabled blind people to read. My interest in the Braille project had nothing to do with Braille. My interest was because Braille workers all lived in barracks eight. Another consideration was that their supervisor, the person technically over the project, was also the unit's classification officer, David Step. If anyone at the unit could get me IB, he was the one who could do it.

Mr. Step frequently ate in staff dining, and one day when he and I were in there alone, I broached the subject with him. "Mr. Step, what would you think about me coming to work for you in Braille?"

"That sounds like a good idea, Allen," he responded. "How much time do you have left?"

"Eighteen years."

"Sounds like a good place for you. Do you have a high school diploma?"

"GED," I replied.

"Get Captain Kenny to give me a call and put you up for classification then we will look at you," Step stated, using that phrase once again that the officers preferred.

I decided that he had been so amiable with my first request that I ought to go ahead and put all my cards on the table. "Mr. Step, what I am really interested in is IB. I know you don't have any IB's working in Braille, but perhaps you would support me for getting on the inmate panel if I do a good job in Braille."

"Yeah, well, we'll look at you; I don't see any problem with that."

I had my foot in the door! Now all I had to do was get Captain Kenny to call Step and put me up for a job change, and I would be on the road to not just one but *two* of my goals.

This second goal is something I had been thinking about for awhile. How could I turn all the crap I have made out of my life into something meaningful? The answer I found is to use my experience to benefit others. Maybe I could help some youngsters see the light before they wrecked their lives like I had wrecked mine. The inmate panel presented a perfect way to do that. They are groups of two to four inmates who go around and speak to junior high and high school students about drugs and prison. I wanted to share my experiences and possibly help steer some youths away from a life of crime and prison.

As time continued to pass, this goal became an obsession and is the reason I am writing this book. As I sit here today, after eighteen years of continuous incarceration, sharing my story is the only way to give my life meaning. Otherwise, my life has been a total waste and I cannot accept that.

In April 1994, I was assigned to the Wrightsville Braille project and started my training to become a Braille typist. Learning Braille is a very complex process in which a person works through a workbook (commonly referred to within the project as the Blue Book) completing exercises on a manual Braille writer. These exercises are designed to teach a step-by-step process until an individual has a grasp of all of Braille's complexities. Every inmate who learns Braille at Wrightsville does so with a project inmate instructor who grades each exercise and determines if the trainee is ready to move on to the next exercise. When all the exercises in the Blue Book are completed, the next step is completing a thirty-five page Braille transcript, also on a manual Braille writer, which is then sent off to the Library of Congress in Washington D.C. for grading. A trainee must make above eighty percent on this manuscript in order to be certified. This entire process takes about sixty days.

I had just completed my manuscript and was working on my first textbook for a blind student when Mr. Step came up to me and said, "Allen, I want you to be the project's clerk. You got any problem with that?"

"No sir, if that is what you want me to do."

"Come on," he said and then walked out of the room.

I followed him to the other room where the clerk and assistant clerk's desks were. Then he announced, "Allen is going to be the clerk, and Smith is going to be his assistant. Anyone got a problem with that? Good. Rush, you and Key train them. This change is effective immediately."

Tim Rush was the current clerk and Steve Key was his assistant. I had heard a little bit about troubles between those two and Mr. Step, but it was not any of my business so I paid it little attention. Little did I know how much it would eventually affect me. I did not like the situation and was very uncomfortable with replacing Rush under what was obviously a hostile atmosphere.

The clerk in the project is a powerful position. It is the only position in which an inmate is actually in charge of a prison office. Even though it was against policy to actually put an inmate in charge of something like an office or program like this, it was widely known and accepted that I ran the program even if all the *official* recognition went to my supervisor.

Mr. Step does not know anything about Braille and he does not work in the project although, he is the direct supervisor for the inmates. Step relies on the clerks to handle every aspect of the day-to-day functions of running the project, including assigning books to be transcribed.

That he had made me, the newest and least informed of the project's inmates, the clerk was ludicrous. At the time, there were thirteen inmates assigned to the project, and, although initial training and some transcription was done on manual Braille writers, the majority of Braille transcription was completed on the project's eight 386 computers. I had never even turned a computer on. How was I to lead this project with such limited knowledge?

Couple my computer ignorance with the fact that Rush also did all the computer maintenance and repair for the project; it was clear to me that I was in way over my head. Additionally, I had never been a clerk before; I did not even know how to type.

I approached Rush as soon as Step had left the room. With so many hurdles to overcome, the first on my list was making myself comfortable with accepting this job, insuring that I was not stepping on Rush's toes.

"Hey, listen, Tim. The last thing I want to do is be any part of you losing your job. If you just say the word, I will tell Step that I can not accept this job."

"Bill, it is not a problem. I quit. He didn't fire me. I refuse to be the clerk for that lying son of a bitch any longer. As a matter of fact, I'll be getting me a job change pretty soon, so you better pay close attention to what I have to teach you."

"Are you sure, man?" I questioned.

"Positive," he responded.

So began my instruction in being the project's clerk. The way Rush had things set up was he and his assistant did the actual computer transcribing of textbooks. The other inmates who were working on computers only did proofreading of the text prior to transcription. Consequently, Rush and Key were the only inmates who were credited with a computer transcription page count, an unrealistic analysis of productivity of the inmate workers. Inmates transcribing on a manual Braille writer were also credited with a page count, but since computer transcription was about ten times faster than manual, it gave the computer transcribers an inflated productivity rating.

Rush was teaching me how to use the Duxbury Braille Program to enter in the codes, which determines the placement of the Braille words on a printed page. I decided that once I learned this process, I would teach the other inmates, who were currently only proofreading scanned, text so they too would be given transcription credits.

Rush started showing me the basics of operating a computer. I was fascinated and totally captivated, and in about ten days I could do some work uninstructed.

Yet, as good as my budding skills were, I was extremely fortunate that Rush did not get his threatened job change for a couple of months, because I also needed to learn something about computer repair. The eight ancient computers offered many opportunities in those couple of months, and by the time Rush's job change materialized, I had learned a few of the fundamentals of computer repair.

Another difficulty was the untenable position of having to supervise the other dozen inmates in the project. Who was I, the person who had been in the project for the least amount of time, to tell another inmate what to do? The practice of one inmate telling another what to do was very much frowned on by inmates themselves. I cannot count the times I have heard some inmate tell another, "You ain't running nothing!"

Yet, I was running something. It was now my responsibility to insure that the books sent to the project from the Arkansas School for the Blind were transcribed in a timely fashion so that they could be sent to the student needing them for school. It was also my responsibility to assign an instructor for new inmates who enter the project and to insure that these two could work together until the trainee was caught up to speed.

The first thing I had to do was show the inmates in the project that it was not my desire to "run anything." So, after quite a lot of thought, I decided to start holding meetings in which any member of the project could voice his opinion concerning the operation of the project or vent any grievance felt toward another member.

I waited until Rush had received his job change and Key had made parole before I called my first meeting. Although both those guys had been helpful in training Smith and me, they were also both disruptive influences within the project. Every time I tried to do something differently, I always got some smart remarks about how that had already been tried and would not work. I do not think either of them intentionally tried to undermine my position. They both had quite a following in the project and Smith and I were both the new guys. Regardless, I waited until both of them were no longer in the project before calling the first meeting.

"Ok, guys. Here's the plan. I did not ask for this clerk job; I am not qualified for it. Don't think I want it or the responsibility, but I am not going to run from it. The thing about it is that I can not do it on my own; I need each and every one of you to help me. If I don't have your help then I will fail. But just because I fail, doesn't mean the project fails. This project is bigger than any one guy, and that is one of Tim Rush's oversights. Tim Rush and Steve Key tried to insure their job security by being the only ones who knew how to work the Duxbury program. They figured that they would never be replaced if no one else knew how to do computer transcription.

"Robert Smith and I have learned how to do Duxbury, and we are going to teach each computer operator how to use it.

"One thing you guys may not be aware of is that every month a monthly report is sent to Step. In this report, it lists the number of Braille pages each of you have done. Previously, the only people who received transcription credit were those on Braille writers or Tim and Steve. All of you who have been proofreading did not receive any credit for your efforts at all. In my way of looking at things, that sucks, and we are going to change it.

"Ok, so we are going to teach everybody on computers how to transcribe, but that's not all. I want to use this venue of meetings for deciding how to run the project. If someone has an idea, they can bring it up in a meeting, and we will discuss it and vote on it. I am not looking to run anything. Of course, as in any operation, there has to be a leader and I have been appointed to that position. I hope that once you see how I plan to lead, I will earn your respect and that you will follow me on your own volition. Any comments?"

"I like what you have said, and I am willing to do whatever it takes to insure that the project is productive," said Rodney Montgomery, one of Braille's longest employed inmates.

"You know," I responded. "We have an amazing opportunity here in the project. We don't work for the ADC or the Wrightsville unit; we work for those blind children whose textbooks we transcribe. We don't even have a supervisor in here with us, and that is unheard of in prison. I think we ought to all really appreciate what we have here and make it the very best Braille transcription institution in the country."

Everyone agreed and the meeting, which I felt like was a one hundred percent success, broke up. I was beginning to feel better about my position and was fortunate to spend the next four and a half years working in the Wrightsville Braille project. It was while working there that I grew into the person I am today.

CHAPTER EIGHTEEN

That May Be Down the Road

The Tao that can be told is not the eternal Tao
The name that can be named is not the eternal name.

Following my mother's visit, came a visit from my sister, April. It is heartening that people are starting to see a different Bill. I do not feel the same as my old self; I feel like life offers opportunities, yes, even opportunities to someone in my dire straits. I had been writing an occasional letter to my father for the last few years and had never received any response. Unknown to me, he had been throwing my letters in the trash upon receipt. However, one letter that I wrote from Wrightsville failed to make the trip to the trash can and wound up on my father's dresser in my parents' bedroom.

One day when my father overheard my mother and sister making plans to come and see me, he happened to remember the letter that he had failed to throw away. Entering his bedroom, he retrieved that letter, sat down on his bed, and read it. My father later told me this story: he realized this letter was written by someone he did not know, written by a different Bill Allen. He was moved by what he read, approached my mother, and asked what he had to do in order to come visit me.

When my mother and sister arrived for the visit, they told me my father wanted to come see me and that I needed to send him a visitation form. To say that I was excited would be an understatement. My father is a stubborn, hard man. He used to tell me that his father whipped his butt every day for things he had done but for which he had not been caught. My mother had always told me the main reason my father and I had such difficulty getting along is that we are so much alike. I do not see the likeness. When hurt by someone, he pushes that person away, and tells himself that he does not care about them. I want to talk and work it out. Perhaps, with the clarity that hindsight provides I can see some of what she was talking about. My father is a fact orientated person, as am I. He is driven to perform to the best of his ability and is very quality conscience. He doesn't ask for help, believing that he can overcome any obstacle on his own. These were parts of my personality that I was just beginning to recognize, yet not ready to omit.

I had been pushed away from my father's affection for many years. I do not blame him in the least for his response; I had hurt him terribly and disappointed him consistently. We all have ways of dealing with pain, and my father's way had worked for him for many years. Pushing me away and denying my existence worked for him. And with someone who delivered as much pain as I had to my family, that was completely understandable. I don't exist, therefore there is no pain associated with me. That he was willing to put himself in harm's way by coming to visit me meant very much. I desperately wanted for him to become aware of the changes in me; I wanted him to know how I had managed to quit drugs. I wanted to impress him. I wanted him to be proud of me, wanted his love. Could I possibly achieve all these things? Only time would tell.

X   X   X

My father did come to see me shortly thereafter. The visit, with my mother and wife also present, was very emotional. My father attempted to remain reserved, but I saw his eyes tear up several times along with mine. I could not push him; the best way for me to prove the changes in me was to be myself. I did not ask for any commitment from him, and the only one he gave was a promise that he would visit again. That was all I could hope for.

After my parents left, Kathy and I discussed the visit and my plans concerning my father in the future. I told her that I would just keep on doing what I am doing; if it is supposed to be, it will be. She made a comment to this statement that was to change my outlook on life even more. She said, "That's a very Taoist attitude."

She had said things like this to me in the past, and rather than show my ignorance, I never questioned her meaning. This time I did, "What do you mean?"

"Do you know what Tao is?" she asked me.

"Never heard of it," I responded.

Kathy proceeded to tell my about this Chinese philosophy/religion/teaching which is five hundred years older than Christianity. I was confused by her explanation but excited by a teaching that seemed to correspond to my way of thinking. Everything seemed to be coming together and the only area in my life in which I felt a void was in my spirituality. I had looked for an avenue for such exploration, but with what I knew of religion and the people involved in it, I did not feel particularly compelled to involve myself with it. The only exception I could apply to the hypocrites who professed to be Christians was my sister.

It is not my desire to preach the teachings of Tao or to even explain it further than to say that it was/is an avenue that I could accept, that could guide me in the search for the truth. It is an inclusive venue that is available for all; it is a teaching that is not an acquirement of knowledge but rather a decreasing of preconceived concepts. I find myself not only uncomfortable with the people who profess the Christian faith but also with its exclusive nature which manifests itself in the doctrine that there is only one way to God: Jesus Christ. I have stated many times that I believe there are many paths up the mountain, but once you get there, the view is the same.

Likewise, it is not my intention to detract from the Christian, or any other faith. All faiths have pathways that lead to the same God. The diversity of the world requires many such paths; otherwise, people like me who search but cannot accept just one teaching, are left without a clear pathway to our Creator.

I have several Christian friends who hope that if I continue to search, my eyes will be opened and I will ultimately accept Christ as my Savior. That may be down the road; I have no idea what the future holds. However, after eighteen years of incarceration, I have seen so many people turn to the Christian faith as a means of escaping the chaos of their own making. This in itself would be understandable, but I have also seen these same people return time after time, pick up the same mantle and continue the cycle. This leaves a bad taste in my mouth, and I cannot bring myself to pursue a similar course while incarcerated. I have only these few difficulties with the Christian faith; I believe it has its merits and offers many millions of people a course which they would otherwise never find.

"It would probably be best if I sent you a copy of the Tao Te Ching, which is kind of like the Taoist Bible," Kathy offered.

Where would I have been without my wonderful wife? What if I had never run my ad in *Spectrum*? I would not be sitting here at Wrightsville, would not be on my way back into the fold of my family, would not be drug free, would not have my meaningful job, and would not have anything at all to live for.

As we talked, my mind had been churning, and I suddenly had a revelation. All my life, whenever I would get into trouble, I could hear my parents say to me, "How could you do this to us?"

I would always respond, "Do what to you? I'm not doing a damn thing to you; this is my life. If I am screwing it up, I am doing it to me, not you!"

I always believed that I was correct in this response. Until this day, I had never had the following revelation: *If someone loves you and you do things that hurt you, it hurts them.* How could I have lived my entire life oblivious to this simple concept?

I do not claim ignorance as a means to excuse the pain I had caused my parents. There is no excuse that can justify bringing such misery into the lives of people whose only interest was what was best for me. Rather, it shows how selfishly I had lived. I do not even think that I had ever loved before. Even with Debbie, it had all just been about me. How could I ever claim love and yet be unfamiliar with this basic concept of love? Coming to this understanding, I vowed something to myself at that time: I would never do anything that would cause my family pain. I realize now that this was a very broad and overzealous commitment, one I would fail to keep. However, my intentions were in the right place, and to this day, this vow guides me in many of my decisions.

My younger brother was the next to come see me, and regular visits from my family followed. I was back in the fold of my family, a family I had rejected through drug abuse, crime, and a total indifference to their concerns.

Through these visits, I would hear about my sister's daughter and my brother's three daughters. This would stir longings within me to meet these little girls, these nieces who had little, if any, idea of an Uncle Bill. Yet, as strong as my desire was to get to know them, I was hesitant because I did not want these girls to know their Uncle Bill as an inmate. I wanted to wait until I got out before I was introduced to them. I was confident of ultimately being released through my appeals. Yet, one day I woke up with the revelation that, although this was not much of a life, it was *my life*, and I should not put things on hold; I needed to live my life to the best of my ability in spite of the situation in which I found myself. Consequently, I decided that I should not wait for my release to meet these little girls. What if my release was many years in the future? I would never get to know these girls as little girls, which would not only be my loss but also theirs.

That evening, I called both my brother and sister and asked them if I could meet their kids. I explained to them my aforementioned thoughts and promised that I would never do anything to hurt them. They both agreed. During the following weeks, I met my nieces; little girls who filled my heart with love and who inspired me in the writing of my first book, *The Cure of the Land*. Their inspiration was farther reaching than the concepts and efforts which went into that endeavor. They were and are a continued stimulus to use my life as a model of what not to do for any youth I can reach through words, written and spoken.

✗ ✗ ✗

Several times, I mentioned to my supervisor, David Step, my desire to get on the inmate panel and one day he called me to his office.

"Allen, Mr. Vincent is looking for someone to be on the inmate panel and I suggested he talk to you. I suggest you go see him."

I thanked Step and went in search of Mr. Vincent, the unit's Grievance Officer and the employee who takes the panel on their trips. Vincent is a mousy little man who talks very softly and gives me the impression that he is scared of his own shadow. When I found him in his office, the first thing he asked me was why I wanted to be on the panel.

I explained my reasons, which seemed to satisfy him, and he took me up front to talk to the warden who approved me. I was ecstatic to have achieved not only one goal but two; I was on the inmate panel, and my class status was upgraded to IB! I felt that I had a story to tell; greatly influenced by my nieces and I wanted to tell it to young people in hopes of opening their eyes so that they never travel down the harrowing path I had traveled. Since I would soon be going to schools to do this, for the first time, I felt like my life could have some meaning.

Additionally, IB meant that in one year I would be eligible for a furlough. To have the opportunity to spend some time with my newfound family was a blessing that I would not take for granted. My past is rife with examples in which I abused the love of my family and took them for granted. It would not happen again! I also had a strong yearning to walk in the woods, to be totally alone, to listen to the quiet. In prison, there is always someone around. Even in the private rooms at Cummins, you knew you were in a barracks with sixty other people, any of which could and quite frequently did, interrupt your solitude. Also, the noise is something to which I have never become accustomed. I wanted so badly to spend time by myself with no other noise than that generated by a forest.

The next day Mr. Vincent called me to his office in the security building and told me that on Thursday of the next week the inmate panel would be going to a high school in Hot Springs to give our talk. I considered and then discarded the idea of preparing a speech. I decided that I would just wing it, speak from the heart. The ten days until our trip could not come fast enough.

I immediately wrote Kathy and my family about the upcoming trip and received replies that were encouraging and supportive. Finally, the day arrived, and as directed, I met Mr. Vincent in the shift briefing room directly across from Braille that morning. I walked up to him and presented myself as ready. His response shattered my dreams.

"Allen, you have been taken off this trip."

"Why?"

"You'll have to talk to the warden about that."

I could tell by his attitude that this was a decision for which there was no appeal, at least not from him, and I returned to Braille despondent. From Braille, I called my supervisor David Step to see if he could shed any light on why I had been removed from the panel trip. His response was guarded, and although I could tell he knew the reason, he was not going to tell me. Basically, he told me the same thing that Vincent had told me, "You'll have to talk to the warden." I asked Step if he could get me up to the warden's office so I could talk to him. His response was, "I'll get back to you." I had learned by this time that this was Step's way to put somebody off, a way to avoid saying, "No".

I had absolutely no idea what was behind my being removed from this panel trip, but I did not think it was something I could not overcome. Obviously, there was some kind of misunderstanding, and whatever it was, I was confident that it could be cleared up. Thinking in this manner, I did not want to do or say anything to any of the parties involved that would have me taken off the panel entirely. I did what I could to find out what was behind this but had no luck. Everybody either expressed ignorance, or they told me that I would have to talk to the warden. The problem was the warden was not someone I could get to unless he wanted to see me. Obviously, he did not.

On Wednesday of the next week, a clerk friend of mine told me that I would be going up before the classification committee. This news encouraged me because the way I had received my class IB was unusual. Generally, class changes are all made through classification. Now that I was going up before the committee, I figured that the reason I had been taken off the Hot Springs panel trip was that I had not been formally classified as IB. Therefore, according to my line of reasoning, I would formally receive class IB on Friday's classification. Consequently, I relaxed and abandoned my efforts to find out what had happened.

On Friday I went to classification, walked into the room where the committee met, and stood before the warden.

"Allen, I guess you have been wondering why you have been taken off the inmate panel?"

"Yes, sir," I responded but was thinking much more. What did he mean "taken off the inmate panel?"

"After placing you on the panel, I instructed that your mail be screened, which is a standard procedure, and a letter you received from your wife caused us some concern that you were planning to escape while on the Hot Springs panel trip." The warden paused here, allowing me a chance to respond. I was struck speechless. This was ludicrous! Kathy had not written me any letter that could be interpreted to mean anything like what he was saying.

"Escape? No, sir! What letter? I have absolutely no idea what you are talking about." Doing a quick mental review of the letters I had received from Kathy, I could not come up with anything that could be considered suspicious.

"A letter where she was asking your advice on some camping equipment for some trip she was planning," the warden answered.

Now I knew what he was talking about but was still confused as to how this letter raised any suspicion. "Sir, my wife went on vacation to Lake DeGray earlier this month with her friends in the Audubon Society. Since she would be camping and since I used to be a Boy Scout and also did a lot of camping with my family when I was younger, she was asking me about what type of tent and sleeping bag she should buy. I don't see how that could raise any eyebrows or be interpreted that I was planning an escape."

"Well, Allen, Hot Springs is a wilderness area, and it is the camping equipment that has caused our concern. Anyway, we will look at it again. For now though, we are reducing you back to class IC. I will talk to you more about this later."

Later never did materialize. The warden never gave me an opportunity to speak to him again about this. However, Kathy did call him, explaining that her vacation had been planned for a month, before we even knew anything about a trip to Hot Springs, and told him she had receipts for this vacation which would prove this is exactly where she went. She sent all the receipts to me along with a detailed letter outlining her activities on her vacation. She even sent a cancelled check for a barge trip she took with the Audubon Society, a trip she had made reservations for a month ago.

I sent copies of all of this to the warden to no avail. Later, I found out the warden was interviewing for a job as the Director of the Department of Correction in Oregon. Although he may have believed me, he was not going to take any chances that an escape might occur from his unit, an escape that could put him in bad light and jeopardize this job opportunity. This event haunted me for years and demolished every attempt to obtain class IB at the Wrightsville unit.

CHAPTER NINETEEN

A Story to Tell

The more laws and restrictions there are, The poorer people become.
The sharper men's weapons, The more trouble in the land.
The more ingenious and clever men are, The more strange things happen.
The more rules and regulations, The more thieves and robbers.

"And so, Ted, you are now up to date on my life," I told my black friend at Wrightsville.

"Have you started your book yet?"

"Yes, I've got the first chapter written. It starts off just like that dream I told you about when we first started this discussion."

"Good. Maybe you can get it published and it will help some people."

"Man, I hope so, but I'm not very confident of my writing ability."

"Don't worry about that; just write it like it happened. Write it like you have told it to me, and someone will recognize it for what it is and help you get it published."

"How long have you been locked up now, Bill?"

"Let's see, it's 1994, since 1984, ten years."

"You ought to start a journal, too. It will help you recall what happens from this point. It will also help get you used to writing and will improve your skills."

"You know, I already planned on doing that and have asked Kathy to send me a book that I can write in."

✗ ✗ ✗

In September of 1994, I had Kathy send me a blank hardback book so I could start my journal. On the 29th of that same month, I started recording my thoughts in what I called "Reflections Beyond a Decade." I have decided to use some excerpts from it in this book. Below is the prose I wrote as an introduction, and following are the entries through the year 1994.

REFLECTIONS BEYOND A DECADE

The passage of days all roll into one. Their increase by number is insignificant. For days, or even years, so poorly measure time where hope is palpable and reality is a mist beyond grasp. Calendars are marked by loved ones lost rather than days gone by. Where silver in a once dark mane, heralds the march of time.

Such is my lot and, although I rue the trail that delivered me thus, little good comes from living in the past. This is why I feel I must write, not of what has been, but of where I find myself today in **Reflections Beyond a Decade**.

9.29.94

This is it. Ten years of continued incarceration. I was asked by a black friend of mine if I wanted something to help me celebrate. I told him that this wasn't anything to celebrate. September 29, 1984—September 29, 1994. Seems like forever, seems like a few months. That's the scary part ... that it can go by so quickly. Here I sit today, thirty-eight years old. In what seems like a few months, will I be sitting here forty-eight years old?

I want to write all of this for two reasons.

1. If I don't manage to get out of here, I don't want to forget how miserable this whole experience has been. I want something to remind me.
2. I'll give this to my wife Kathy. She knows me so well, she knows me so little. I offer her this so she can know the Bill Allen that she doesn't see during our once a week, four hour visit.

Today is at an end. Nothing special. Rodney David and Dan Evans decided that they would like to start working out with me so I changed my schedule to evenings. They both did pretty good for the first day. We'll see how long they hang.

Well, to my book, to my radio and then, to bed so I can rise tomorrow and face day 3652.

10.02.94

To my little sister is born a son, to me a nephew, David Allen Dennis, born 9/30/94 at 4:15 p.m. To me this birth represents a strengthening of my faith that there is indeed a God that concerns Himself with our little lives. I've never really been concerned about a birth before, until this one. I've never prayed so fervently for anything before. I don't think that God looked down saying, "I wasn't going to let this be a complication free birth, but since Bill Allen is praying for it, I guess I will." That is immaterial. It matters not whose prayer God answered, because I know there were many, the fact remains that the prayer was answered!

I've got four nieces and now three nephews. I've never seen any of them and with the birth of David, I wonder when or if I'll ever get to see him. I said jokingly to Kathy yesterday on visit, "David can come give me a ride home when I get out." Kathy didn't appreciate the joke.

Welcome to the world David. I wish you health and happiness!
Cowboys beat Washington today! 34-7

10.07.94

We were having some trouble in Braille. People were coming in and playing on the computers. It was really getting out of hand and I was faced with a dilemma in how to deal with it. If I tried to tell the people working there that all the traffic had to stop, then I may very well have had to fight. If I went to the folks about the problem, I'd be a snitch. If I let it continue, sooner or later there would be problems.

I decided to call a meeting, a bitch session. Let the guys complain about whatever they wanted, hoping that someone would bring up the traffic problems. Someone did and we all discussed it. The outcome was just what I hoped it would be. And the best thing about it was that nobody suspected that was the reason that I called the meeting. They thought it was their idea. For the last two days very few people have come in and now the word is out "Braille is off limits!"

10.09.94

I was just sitting here wondering how is it that day after day I keep what can only be termed a "good attitude?"

Yes, I have a lot of things going for me, my wife, my family, my appeal. But still ... there are so many things about freedom that I miss so much. Is it faith that keeps me going? Is it hope? Fear? Or am I becoming institutionalized?

I truly don't know and that bothers me some. How am I so certain that I'll never quit trying to obtain my freedom, that I'll continue to try to better myself so that I'll be prepared for freedom when I obtain it? For, I am sure! Is this the strength and faith I've prayed for? The changes that so many others have prayed for? So many questions, so few answers.

10.16.94

It has been a week since my last entry. I believe I've been waiting for my attitude to change, for some negative emotions, depression or the like. But I feel good. Nay GREAT!

The relationship with my wife couldn't be better. She has decided to go on a diet without any prompting from me and she really looks great. Visits have been wonderful, no money problems, nothing negative at all. Kathy amazes me with her determination in her struggle with OCD and determination to be supportive and helpful with me. Her every action speaks volumes of her love for me. I love her so.

Work has been great, too! Mr. Step has called on me to help him prepare an orientation package for new arrivals and seems really pleased and supportive of everything I'm doing in Braille. The Cowboys are even kicking butt all over the NFL.

Life is sweet, if only I was free!

10.21.94

Kids are so wonderful! Tonight I received a letter from my niece, Renee. When I saw the pink envelope with the little animals on it, my mood was immediately lifted. In several of my letters to her I've called her "Princess." In tonight's letter she called me "Prince." That's priceless!

11.12.94

So many things going on and I've been remiss in making entries.

Two weeks ago I stormed out of visit on Kathy. She made me mad and as usual my anger flashed and I left. I didn't write her all that week and to my surprise she didn't write me. Then last week she didn't show up for visit.

As usual with me, I started preparing myself for her to leave me. This is something I have noticed repeatedly. Whenever there is a conflict with someone, or just an imagined conflict, I start preparing myself to be abandoned. I think I start thinking like that so I never find myself begging for someone not to abandon me. In other words, if that is what they want, then I prepare myself to accept it without pleading and thereby causing them to remain with me through guilt. It seems very important to me that my family do what they do with me "because they want to," maybe too important. I think this because, of all the times I have prepared myself to be abandoned, nobody has even considered it. What to do? Lower my standards?

It has become a very real possibility that I may be parole eligible soon! I went up to the records office Monday to review my jacket. Afterwards, I was talking to Rodney Montgomery about the dates of my crime and when I was to expire my parole from my old sentence. Rodney explained to me that regardless of when I was sentenced on this charge, the fact that it was committed while I was on parole means that my time must be computed starting back in 1976 under the parole eligibility laws in effect at that time.

The result of all of this would be that I'm many years past my parole eligibility date, five to seven years past. I wrote the records supervisor here at Wrightsville and sent her these dates and my interpretation of them and asked her to re-compute my time. Thursday, she reviewed my jacket and couldn't kill my interpretation and so forwarded it to her supervisor in Pine Bluff.

I am trying to refrain from getting too excited about this but it's very difficult. This could change so much for me. I'm forced to look at doing time in a whole different light. A whole new ball game with new rules.

I'm looking at the possibility of being free, being with my wife, my parents, my family, my nieces. OVERWHELMING!

Kathy should be here today and I'll be able to share my excitement with her. I hesitate to do so because I don't want her to get let down again. But I believe this will happen; it feels right.

I've prayed that God prepare me for this. I'm confident that I'm ready for freedom. I won't be back! My only concern is my temper.

11.24.94

Thanksgiving. I really hate the holidays. They always leave me feeling what all I can't do, like be with my family. Last year was a little different because it was the first holiday season that I was in the good graces of my family. It is a little early to tell how I feel this year. Today Kathy is eating Thanksgiving dinner at Jason's (my brother) with all my family. I know that I am thankful for my family. I wish I could be with them today!

The records supervisor is giving me some problems on computing my parole eligibility like I believe it should be. I'll probably have to take them to court.

On the twenty-second I received my brief that is filed in Eighth Circuit Court of Appeals. A ruling from that should come down in February. I'll probably wait until that is decided before I take this parole issue to court. I don't look forward to the fight or expense. However, if I have to, I will. Can't just give up and accept the next eighteen years.

11.26.94

Visit today. Oh what a wonderful visit! Mom and Dad were here and really amazed me. Dad said that ten years ago he took me out of his will. Last week he went to see his lawyer and revised his will to set up a trust fund where I would receive one-quarter of their estate upon their deaths.

To say that the money this represents means nothing to me would be a lie. I've considered the future. If Kathy leaves me and my parents die and I'm still in here, how would I survive? I can't go back to my old hustle. But now I know how I'd survive. Yes, this is a very selfish position but how could I not look towards that bleak possibility? I've still got eighteen calendar years to do!

Yet, let me get away from such heartless calculations. God forbid that my parents die while I'm still in here, that I'm never able to spend any time with them. And God forbid that my marriage fold without my being able to show Kathy that all her suffering and loneliness was for a good cause.

World, it felt wonderful to know that my parents believe in me, see my change and approve of me. Not in my wildest imagination did I ever expect for them to believe in me so completely without me spending years and years out in the world proving myself over and over again. This is what means more to me than anything else. Oh now Lord, if I could only get out there and be with my family!

Mom told me how Renee has all my letters saved in a little jewel box and how Renee said, "What I love to do is read them all over and over." This little girl has touched my heart in a way that nobody ever has. I'd die before I ever hurt her!

12.18.94

Do the citizens of this country really wonder at its slip into decadence? I think not, for it is apparent for all to see. Yet, it seems that even the seeing all turn a blind eye at its cause and would rather cite the effects; drug abuse, crime and suicide. Yes, these are just effects. What has turned teens to drug abuse, crime and suicide? That is what must be faced. Why is there no respect for law in the teens of today? Perhaps it is because there is no respect for the law by our leaders of today.

Just in the last week the number three man in the Justice Department has resigned and pled guilty to two felony charges. The President of the United States, Bill Clinton, stands to be indicted in relation to Whitewater. The Governor of Arkansas, Jim Guy Tucker, faces possible indictment in regards to a failed savings and loan. The Secretary of State of Arkansas, Bill McCuen is involved with a flag scandal that could bring about criminal charges. Even the former Attorney General, Steve Clark, the man whose name is on all my state appeals, opposing my release, had to resign in disgrace after being convicted of felonies.

How can kids hold respect for the law when these are the public servants held in example? The bad laws in this country also teach disrespect for all laws. I'll use the drug laws as an example.

Our government has promoted upon a campaign for almost two decades to eradicate drug use. It has failed miserably. Yet why they thought it would work is beyond me. Prohibition failed, drug wars have failed.

Large portions of this country's citizens choose to use drugs, whether it is a social toot, a joint or a hell-bent junkie. They have made their choice. Many of these are parents who through their choice demonstrate to their kids a disregard for the law. Nothing will halt the slip into decadence until the focus is placed on the cause rather than the effect. No problem is ever solved until it is identified. Identify the problem and the solution will lay just around the corner. However, our government leaders are much better at pointing the finger at others rather than themselves. Thus, the solution remains elusive.

12.25.94

It's Christmas morning. This is one day of the year I hate the most. A close second is one week away ... my birthday.

I haven't much liked Christmas since I was a kid. My memories of it, as a child, are all fond but, as an adult, it always represents a time of year that I'm never with my family. It is a lonely time of year and one I'm always grateful when over. This year is no exception.

I will see Kathy today and possibly my parents but I don't even really look forward to that. It must be a real bummer to come to prison to visit on Christmas. I wish I could call off visit.

I received the state's reply to my appeal in the Eighth Circuit Court of Appeals. Reading those state responses is depressing. I have instructed my attorney how I want him to reply. Our last filing is due 1/5/95. From that point a ruling should be forthwith. I'm ready. In the past, I have always wanted the court's rulings but also didn't want them. At least while I am waiting on a ruling, hope is still alive. But now I want this ruling quickly. I have waited long enough. I want to know where I stand.

A friend of mine Chuck James arrived here the other day and is in my barracks. Even he is amazed at the change in me. We used to sleep beside each other when I was acting a fool down in barracks nine, six and seven years ago.

12.26.94

Finally, Christmas is over! My parents and Kathy did show up for visit yesterday and it was nice. I'm glad that I was unable to cancel it yesterday. My parents didn't really have anything better to do yesterday as the normal Christmas schedule was thrown off by the family all going different directions for Christmas. Today they (including Kathy) are all gathering at April's for Christmas dinner. That ought to be still going on as I write. Oh, how I wish I was there! At least Kathy is there for me.

Kathy made a special effort yesterday to let me know that she loves me dearly. Her efforts had her desired effect... I feel loved!

Now the march of time continues as my thirty-ninth birthday approaches. Lord how long will this nightmare continue?

My parents are considering helping me obtain a 309 (A program where state inmates are housed in county jails). Kathy is also ready to embark on this project. Now is the time I need to look towards 1995 and set my goals. What are the possibilities? 309, State Police Headquarters, habeas relief, start clemency process. For 309 I need to compile an information packet about myself for my parents and Kathy to use in my behalf. I'll start on that tomorrow.

Everything that can be done is done concerning my habeas corpus. I'll have to knuckle down on my parole eligibility issue and probably get that filed in court.

So my goals are as follows:

GOALS FOR 1995

1. *Do everything possible for 309.*
2. *Follow up on parole eligibility, including filing in court if necessary.*
3. *Continue to improve the Braille Program and seek Mr. Steps' help in a transfer to the State Police Headquarters.*
4. *Maintain clean disciplinary record.*
5. *Give the inmate panel another go.*
6. *If denied in Eighth Circuit, file an appeal to the U.S. Supreme Court.*
7. *Never let Kathy doubt how much I love and appreciate her.*

CHAPTER TWENTY

Prepared for Disappointment

It is not wise to rush about.

The ensuing years at Wrightsville proved to be beneficial to my growth, although there were many ups and downs. I have come to view the downs in life equally as important as the ups, if not more so. It is through adversity that one grows. The year 1995 saw the denial of my appeal, and, although this was a major blow that affected my entire future, I came to terms with it and continued to prosper. That same year, the ADC installed a collect call telephone system for use by the inmates. This was a big bonus and aided Kathy and I greatly in our struggle to maintain a marriage under such severe circumstances. It also allowed me to talk to my young nieces whose presence in my life through this medium and letter writing was a blessing that continued to influence me.

In 1996, my brother, Jason, and sister started bringing my nieces to visit me, and The *Cure of the Land* was completed. Additionally, that year revealed that the inmate panel was not going to be a reality. I had pushed as hard as I possibly could to obtain IB trustee status, and every effort had proved vain. Finally, at the end of my rope, I approached Mr. Step and asked him the same question I had been asking various people for six years, "What do I have to do to get IB?"

Mr. Step responded, "Allen, I will make a deal with you. It's January 1996; if you stay my clerk in Braille for two more years, I will get you IB at the end of that time. Six months later, I will send you to the State Police Headquarters."

Two more years! This was a difficult pill to swallow, but one I managed to choke down. The fact was I had nothing more promising on the horizon. With the denial of my appeal, the only possible promise for the future was clemency, a pipe dream at best. Consequently, I had come to face the fact that I had many more years of incarceration ahead of me. Thus thinking, I accepted Step's proposal.

My marriage to Kathy ended in 1997. She simply got tired of waiting for me to come home. Fortunately, I had entered SATP (Substance Abuse Treatment Program) prior to our breakup. I do n't know if I would have fallen off my sobriety wagon without the information I learned in the program, but I do know it was a close call.

Initially, I had entered SATP as an enhancement to my record prior to a clemency bid. There was a new Governor in office, Mike Huckabee, and he was granting clemency to deserving inmates. With this new governor, clemency was no longer a pipe dream but a real possibility. As I worked toward that goal, SATP seemed like a good direction. I entered the program with the attitude, "Nobody can tell me about drugs; I know everything about how to get off drugs."

I had been off the needle for seven years and had not smoked a joint or had a drink in over four years. However, after just a few days in the program, I thought, "You are going to have to spend thirty days living in this program. You might as well go ahead and listen rather than just going through the motions."

It was through this revision of attitude that I became aware of the role of pain in a substance abuser's life. Drug abusers numb pain with drugs or use them to escape from it. We never face the pain or deal with it directly; consequently, when the high wears off, the pain is still present. Thus starts another cycle of never-ending abuse. I found out that I must first experience the pain, knowing the full anguish of the pain. Only then could I accept that I had survived it. Only by fully accepting the worst depths of pain, could I shake the control that pain formerly had over me. I remember telling myself that I had faced the worst pain of my life—much of it I had brought on myself (and on loved ones as well as victims I did not know)—but *I was still standing.* Another bit of knowledge I learned in that program that directly aided me in maintaining sobriety after Kathy and I broke up concerned the use of a Higher Power to aid me when desire to escape my pain through smoking marijuana almost overwhelmed me. I learned that when such desire hit that I could simply ask God to take it away and, miraculously, the desire would evaporate. I utilized this method and what I had learned about pain to stay clean many times throughout the months of our divorce. Although my opinion of God at this point was still up in the air, I had no doubt that there was a creator and that He has more power than me. I utilized this method and what I had learned about pain to stay clean many times throughout the months of our divorce. Once again, I gave thanks that I had not been released prior to learning these two crucial lessons. However, now I was really ready for freedom, and the following year promised to bring it.

✗ ✗ ✗

In January of 1998, I presented myself to Mr. Step in his office, told him I had fulfilled my part of our bargain and had remained his clerk in Braille for the required additional two years and was now ready for him to assist me in getting IB status. Mr. Step looked at me with a confused expression on his face and replied, "Allen, I never promised you IB."

I was astounded and related to him verbatim our conversation of two years ago. He told me that I had misunderstood him. The first thing that came to my mind was how Tim Rush, the clerk I had replaced in Braille, had warned me that Step would screw me around, that he was a liar. Now I had the proof sitting there in front of me, and I left his office more angry than I remember being in a long while. I made a decision on that day that I have subsequently come to regret many times over the following years. I would remain in Braille throughout the upcoming bid for clemency, but that was it. If I failed to make clemency, I would not work for this man any longer.

The chances of receiving clemency grew and grew as I witnessed many people I had known receive it and be freed. Additionally, my father and sister became very active in supporting me for release. They both started contacting people that they knew who either knew parole board members or the governor and laid the groundwork for a successful hearing and ultimate release. Both wrote letters of recommendation and assisted me in obtaining letters from many others who, through their efforts, decided to support me.

One question asked me by my father brought about one of the most favorable aspects of possibly being granted clemency: "What are you going to do about employment?"

I was not particularly concerned about a job or stating that I had employment possibilities in my clemency petition. I knew that with my computer and Braille skills I had something that was marketable in the world. Additionally, I did not see how anyone considering my release could fault me for not having a job lined up after being incarcerated for fourteen years. However, I remembered one tour that I had conducted in the Braille project for some visiting dignitaries from the blind community in the state of Arkansas. There was one blind man who was the Director of the Services for the Blind in the Department of Human Services. At the conclusion of the tour, he had approached me and stated, "Upon your release, if you need a job, contact me." He then gave me his card.

I found his card and wrote Jim Head a letter asking him if he remembered me and if he would consider writing a letter stating that he would consider hiring me if I was granted clemency. His response was more than I had hoped. He definitely remembered me, and, not only would he consider hiring me, he sent me an application for employment with the Services of the Blind as a Braille and Recording Specialist. He told me to fill out the application and return it to him as soon as possible.

I was astounded when shortly thereafter Mr. Step called me and told me that he was transferring a call from Jim Head. Mr. Head then told me that it was necessary for me to be interviewed for the job, but, that considering the situation; this interview could be conducted by phone. He asked me to call his assistant the following week, and she would conduct the interview. I made the call and was hired. I could not believe it! Here I was a state inmate being hired by the biggest state agency! Beyond hiring me, Mr. Head and his assistant requested to appear at my clemency hearing so that they could tell the parole board that I was working for them. The only condition was that I had to be granted clemency.

My father and sister had been visiting with the assistant chairperson on the parole board, Debbie Summer, and had secured a hearing for me, which would be held in June of 1998. Ben Bowie, the State Coordinator at the Arkansas School for the Blind, also planned to appear at the hearing. Ben was founder of the Braille project and someone with whom I had worked closely all my years in Braille. He is a person I deeply respect. Ben also wrote a moving letter to file with my petition.

During this period of my life, I did an evaluation of my past and possible future, mentally juxtaposing the two. I considered the people I had hurt and the crimes I had committed of which I had never been convicted. I looked at who I am today and my wish to use my past to benefit people. I accepted the fact that although I never physically hurt anyone in a robbery, I terrified many innocent victims, not all of them pharmacists. I realized that it must be a terrible trauma to be under the gun of a drug-crazed maniac. I have prayed for forgiveness for all the pain I had brought my family and victims. I hope that by remaining drug free and helping others I can somehow atone for my past.

An honest appraisal found me ready for the responsibilities of freedom but struggling with the concept of deserving clemency. I realized that to the average citizen my crimes would warrant incarceration for life. Yet, is not our criminal justice system designed around rehabilitation rather than punishment? If the purpose of my sentence was to rehabilitate me, the ends of justice have been served. I will never do drugs or commit any criminal act again. As for deserving clemency, I believe that it is only through the grace of God that I will someday walk out of these gates. I do not believe that there is anything favorable I have done in my past, or will do in the future, which can make me stand up and say, "I deserve this!"

As I prepared for my hearing, I also prepared for disappointment and the necessity of new employment at Wrightsville in case my petition was rejected. I had good relations with all the supervisors on the unit, and I could have any clerk job I wanted. I had made it a policy to assist any area that had computer problems and, by doing so, had been offered many jobs which I always graciously refused. What job could compare to the project?

One day, I went to the business office in the security building to pick up some office supplies and while there saw the business manager, Teri Beck, with an open ledger book on her desk, entering in columns of numbers.

"Do you mind if I ask what you are doing?" I questioned her.

"I'm logging expenditures from my budget."

I noticed she had a computer on her desk and wondered why she would use obsolete means to keep financial records when she had a computer at her disposal.

"Why don't you use your computer?"

"I don't know how to do it on a computer."

"Listen, I can help you. I've built several databases, and I could build you one that would keep up with all of those records plus much more."

So started my involvement in the business office and my association with one of the finest people I have ever known. I started spending a lot of time in the business office constructing the database, which was my most comprehensive effort in this area to date. Eventually, I asked Mrs. Beck if she would like to have me for a clerk if I failed to win release in my upcoming clemency bid. Without any hesitation, she agreed.

On the day of my hearing, my entire family, with the exception of my older brother's family who live in Louisiana, Ben Bowie from the Arkansas School for the Blind, Jim Head, and Kathy Moss, his assistant from the Services for the Blind, were all in attendance to support my cause.

We were fortunate that the parole board member who was conducting the hearing was the chairman of the board, Mr. Benson. As we all took our seats in the room, he asked me why I should be granted clemency. I told him of my efforts and success getting off drugs, how I had learned to accept responsibility for my actions, and how I had matured over the fourteen years I had been incarcerated. I talked for approximately five minutes and ended by stating that, if granted clemency, no one would ever have cause to regret it.

My father spoke next and told of our past relationship. He said that he had believed prisoners should serve their entire sentence. Now he realized that I was a different person, so he supports me one hundred percent. He said if I was released he would do everything within his power to assist me.

Ben Bowie spoke of my work in the Braille project and his total support of me and my release. Jim Head told Mr. Benson that I had been hired as a Braille and Recording Specialist and that if released today would have a job working for the state this afternoon.

Mr. Benson looked through my jacket and then spoke to me, "Allen, this is exactly the type of case we are looking for. I want to explain to you what your responsibilities will be when you are released. You not only have a responsibility to the state and to all these fine people to stay out of trouble and make something out of your life, but also to all the inmates who will be applying for clemency. You have to go out there and do well, or it will hurt their chances."

The hearing ended on a positive note, and not one person who attended doubted that I would be granted clemency. All that was left now was to wait. The board would gather in one week, review my petition, and cast their vote. If they found my petition to be with merit, it would be passed on to the governor with their recommendation. It would also be forwarded to the governor if they determined it was without merit, but the governor had made it clear to the entire state that he would follow his board's recommendation.

I spent most of my week waiting and working in the business office, determined that I was through with David Step. The day after the board met and voted, Mrs. Beck made a call to Central Office to find out the results of my hearing. When she returned to her office and I looked up from the computer, I saw tears in her eyes and knew she had bad news. The board had rejected my petition.

X   X   X

I was assigned as the business office clerk on July 5, 1998, a job that would lead to so much inmate jealousy that my entire world would soon come crashing down. Mrs. Beck had recently become the sponsor for an organization called the inmate counsel. This group's entire purpose was to improve the quality of life for inmates at the Wrightsville Unit. She asked me if I would like to take part in the counsel. I told her that in the past I had seen many inmate counsels and that, although their purpose was to improve every inmate's life, they were just a bunch of self-serving hypocrites. She was appalled that I would think this way about anything in which she was directly involved and eventually convinced me to look at this counsel with an open mind. I agreed solely because she was the sponsor.

After watching them for about a month, I decided to join; when a vacancy came up for the office of president, I ran and won. I was able to utilize the leadership skills I had developed in Braille to run the council. Personally, it seemed that it was the best counsel in the entire ADC.

The most rewarding aspect of this time period was that I was allowed to start speaking to tours of school children visiting Wrightsville. Since every effort to obtain IB and get on the inmate panel had been foiled, addressing tours was an acceptable and rewarding alternative. Due to the fact that the kids in these tours came from different venues, some from public school, others from court-imposed programs, I had varying talks. One was a rough styled program for those kids already on the wrong road, and the other was the story of how I ended up in prison that sought to be preventative.

In November 1998, a group of youths from a court-imposed program visited the unit and were escorted by a security officer to barracks two, an empty barracks since everyone who lived there was out to work. Prior to their arrival, I obtained permission from the warden to use a couple of the prisoner made shanks (knives) that were in a display case in his office for the talk. I selected a couple of the vilest looking specimens available. One was an ice pick styled weapon, and the other was a fourteen inch long sword made from a lawnmower blade with a wooden handle. This shank had a wood sheath and looked like a stick when the two pieces were together. I also asked a security officer if he had a five dollar bill I could use in my demonstration. That I was afforded these props to use in my talk even impressed me with the degree of trust that I was afforded. Had I injured one of these children with these contraband items, the Department of Correction would still be trying to dig its way out of the ensuing law suits. However, hurting anyone was the furthest thing from my mind.

When I entered barracks two, all the children were gathered in the day room and were sitting on the benches the inmates who lived in this barracks used for watching TV. I noticed that the entire group was male, and I walked over to the group supervisor and asked in a tone low enough that the kids could not hear me, "I have two kind of talks: one is easy and the other is pretty rough. Which would you like for me to give?"

"Give them the rough one; these kids are pretty rough themselves."

I looked at the children sitting quietly before me and only saw boys aged twelve to fifteen who looked anything but rough to my calloused eye. The four benches they were all crammed together on were lined up one behind the other and turned so they faced the center of the dayroom. I walked up, stood directly in front of them, and asked, "How many tough guys do we have in this group?"

They all just sat there meekly staring at me. "Come on, assholes. This is supposed to be the cream of the upcoming criminal crop, and there aren't any tough guys in here?"

Finally, one fat boy sitting on the front bench raised his hand. "Oh, so there is at least one tough guy, huh?" I asked as I walked and stood before him, my right hand in my pocket where the ice pick shank was hidden. "Well, tough guy, do you think you could handle me?"

This brown-headed, overweight boy looked me up and down insolently and said, "Yeah, I think I could take you."

"Well, get on up fat boy and show me what you can do," I responded, stepping back a step to allow him room to rise and at the same time pulling the ice pick from my pocket.

He started to rise, then saw the weapon I was holding down at my side, immediately sat back down, and exclaimed, "Hell no! You have a weapon!"

"Sure, I have a weapon; you think in prison we worry about fair fights? Come on, fat boy!"

"Nah, that's all right. I'll pass."

"Ok, I'll lose the knife," I slid the knife on the floor towards the prison guard who looked relieved that I had relinquished the weapon.

"How about now, fat boy?" I prompted my victim.

Again, he started to rise, and this time I reached under the back of my shirt, pulled what looked like a stick out from down the back of my pants, and gave a violent shake of my wrist which sent the sheath flying across the room, exposing the fourteen inches of hard steel shank I had in my hand. The boy's eyes became as large as saucers, and he almost fell over backwards on the bench.

"Hell no, man! You don't play fair!"

"What do you think happens in prison, punk? You think we are concerned about rules of fair fighting? We commit felonies to get in here; you think we are worried about rules. Sit down, punk. You don't have any business trying me."

"Prison is a place where hope is consumed by despair. Each of you has been placed by the courts in the program which brought you down here. The next stop on your agenda is not a visit here but to be sentenced here. I know I was, when I was your age, taken on a visit of the Tucker unit. I guess I liked it so much that in 1976 I was sentenced there for ten years for three armed robberies of drug stores. I guess

I liked that enough that in 1984 I was sentenced to fifty years without parole for another pharmacy robbery."

"How many of you were born after September 29, 1984?"

Three quarters of the hands were raised. "Every step you have ever taken, every thought you have ever had, every word you have ever spoken, every day of your entire life, I have been here and let me tell you, here sucks."

I went on to tell them of the deaths I had witnessed, the person I have seen set on fire, all the violence which is the regular fare in prison. I wanted to impress on these kids that prison was not a cool place to be but a place from which you may not leave alive. I also touched on the games which are played on new arrivals to trick them into becoming submissive to the predators which stalk prison barracks.

I had folded up the five dollar bill into a small square, and, as I talked about these games, I approached a slight blond boy sitting on the corner of the front bench. "Here, hold onto this for a minute, would you?" Pretending like I was trying to be secretive, I spoke low and handed this bill to him cupped in my hand. He took it and held it in his open hand which rested on his lap.

"No, damn it," I rebuked him in a low and harsh voice. "Put it in your pocket!"

He quickly complied with my instruction, and I continued with my talk. After about ten minutes, I approached the boy I had given the bill and told him, "Ok, let me have that now."

He dug in his pocket and handed me back the same folded up bill; I thanked him, turned, and started walking away. As I did so, I unfolded the bill, looked at it, quickly turned around, rushed back to stand right in front of this boy, and exclaimed, "Hey, asshole. Where is the money I gave you?"

"That's it," answered the now frightened kid.

"The hell it is. I gave you a fifty dollar bill, and you are going to try giving me back five bucks. Give me my fifty dollars!" I demanded, holding out my hand.

The poor kid started shaking; I thought for a minute that he was going to cry, and I decided to let him off the hook. "Those are the games we play."

After my talk, I took the kids on a tour of the barracks. My favorite place to take them was the bathroom because in this room I could paint a particularly distressing picture. The bathroom had two toilets, a urinal, two showers, and two sinks. I would place a person by each toilet, one facing the urinal, one in each shower, and another by a sink; then, I would take the boy I had identified the most sensitive, place him by a sink, and tell him, "Ok, you are getting up and have to get ready for work and enter the bathroom to brush your teeth. The facilities are full; you've even got two people over here taking craps as you brush your teeth. Have you ever tried breathing through your mouth as you brush your teeth? In prison, you get used to it, that or get used to the smell of shit while you brush."

I turned to the guys standing by the toilets and asked, "Have you ever had to wipe your ass with an audience?"

Both boys shook their heads, and I turned to the entire group and stated,

"There is no privacy in prison. When you enter here, you toss privacy out the window. If you pick your nose, somebody is going to be watching."

I enjoyed talking to the tours and continued to do so for the remainder of my time at Wrightsville, which would not be much longer.

Ultimately, inmates started writing letters about Mrs. Beck and me, suggesting that we had much more going on than a clerk/supervisor or president/sponsor relationship. In order to cease the rumors, the powers that be decided they would transfer me. In May of 1999, I found myself back at the Cummins Unit and working in staff dining.

CHAPTER TWENTY-ONE

"Mom, Are You Sitting Down?"

In every adversity there is the seed of
an equivalent or greater benefit.

The ensuing years were difficult to endure. I found myself back at my starting point, staff dining at Cummins, and then transferred to two other units within the Department of Correction. However, my goals remained the same as I continued to pursue class IB and clemency.

In January of 2001, I was transferred to the Tucker Unit and began working as fire and safety clerk. That May, a friend who was serving a life sentence asked if I wanted to come to work with him as a clerk at outside maintenance. His supervisor requested my reassignment, and I went before the Classification Committee and was granted the job change and IB status.

Finally, I had achieved one of my goals and could not help but be excited at the prospect of possibly acquiring my tandem aim of clemency. My efforts in this direction doubled as the possibility of achievement loomed. My sister became active in the pursuit of my clemency, and, although I did not see how the case I had put together in 1998 could be equaled, my hope did not diminish.

With two years of trustee status under my belt and letters of recommendation from a prosecuting attorney, sheriff, chief of police, and firm commitments from the parole board acquired by my sister, I filed for clemency again in May of 2003. Once again, the waiting began.

✗ ✗ ✗

Six months later, as was my habit at 8:00 p.m. on weeknights, I was lying on my bed at the Tucker Unit listening through my headphones to *Get the Led Out* (three Led Zeppelin songs played in a row on FM radio station Magic 105). A guard came up to my room and told me there was some legal mail for me at Master Control.

Since it was the only thing I had going which was in any way of a legal nature, I figured that it must concern clemency. Butterflies danced in my stomach as I walked down the hallway to Master Control. Either I was going to get the best news of my life or was going to have to face the fact that there were nine more years before my sentence was complete.

When I arrived at Master Control, the officer handed me a manila envelope, and I immediately looked at the return address. It was from the office of the governor. I turned and was going to carry it back to the barracks so that I could open it in private, but the officer at Master Control told me, "You have to open it here, Allen, and show me that there is no contraband in it."

"Yeah, right. The Governor of Arkansas is going to be sending me contraband!" I responded.

"That is the rules."

What was the point of arguing? I ripped the end off the envelope, pulled the document from it, and showed the officer that the governor had not sent me any dope or cigarettes. The document looked like a certificate, and, as I perused it, the impact of its import almost caused me to fall on my face. In bold type across the top, it said, "Certificate of Executive Clemency." I stopped, standing right in the middle of the hallway, and read that my time had been cut by the Governor of Arkansas to a term of thirty-four and a half years and ordered the Department of Correction to release me immediately.

"Allen, get out of the middle of the hallway!" yelled the guard.

I was so dazed that I could only respond, "Yes, sir."

Somehow, I made it back to my abode; I do not even remember the walk. As I entered the barracks, I approached the inmate collect call telephones and immediately paused to dial my mother's phone number.

"Hello," my mother answered.

"Mom, are you sitting down?"

"Yes, why?"

"Mom, I made clemency! The governor cut my time to thirty-four and one-half years and ordered the ADC to release me immediately. Mom, I'm coming home!"

"Why, son, that is fantastic!" I heard her calling for my father saying, "Jake, Jake, Bill made clemency and is coming home!" I could tell now that my mother was crying, and this tough old convict joined her in shedding tears of happiness.

"Mom, I don't know just when it will be; it will probably take a couple of days for them to process the paperwork and cut me loose. Don't call April. I want to call her right now and tell her myself."

"Of course, son. Congratulations, Bill. I am so very happy and proud of you!"

"Thank you, Mom. I'll call just as soon as I learn more. I love you!"

"I love you too, Bill. Goodbye."

Next, I called my sister. The phone was answered by my nephew who went to find his mother after telling his Uncle Bill about a recent victory in softball.

"Hi there," my sister said as she picked up the phone.

"Hi, yourself. April, I made clemency! The governor cut my time to thirty-four and one-half years and ordered the ADC to release me immediately. April, I'm coming home!"

"Oh, Bill, that is great! When?"

"I don't know. The paperwork I got from the governor says 'immediately', probably though, it will take a couple of days for the records office to get notified and process me out. Well, Sis, it doesn't look like David is going to get to come get me. Maybe you can bring him with you when you come down."

"Just let me know when to come, and we will be there. Congratulations, Bill. I am so pleased for you!"

"Thank you, April. I'll give you a call when I know more. I love you!"

"I love you, too. Goodbye."

As I made my way to my room, I encountered a friend, showed him the clemency certificate, received his congratulations, and then went to lie on my bed. I was still dazed; nineteen years of incarceration was about to come to an end, and I was having trouble grasping the idea of it. However, I was not given much time for reflecting on my good fortune as word quickly spread through the barracks that Bill Allen had been granted clemency and was about to be released. There was a steady stream of well-wishers and those who wanted to be in the close proximity of someone so fortunate.

I went to bed when the guard called, "Lights out!" at 10:30 p.m., but it was hours later when I finally managed to get to sleep. I spent those hours thanking God and going over my plans. There was no way that I was going to fall into the same trap which so many ex-cons are lured; the speed trap was enough for me. I was not going to return! I would not revert to drinking and drugs. I had learned how to live my life without the use of drugs, and I knew that there was not one thing I would encounter in the world which would cause me to retreat to their use.

My dreams were finally coming true; I was going to be free! I would be living with my sister and would have to quickly find a job so that for the first time in many years, Bill could take care of himself. I was excited about finally being able to go into schools, talk to kids, telling them about the "speed trap," and using my almost twenty years of incarceration as the foundation for my lectures about a path they did not want to follow.

The next morning while at work, I was called by the records office and told to appear so that they could process me out. I was leaving today! I could not believe it; I was going to get out of prison today!

I made the journey to inside the prison from my office outside the fence in record time. Everybody I encountered on my trek, I told, "I'm going home right now!" By the time I got to the back door of the unit and entered the prison proper, I had a following of about twenty inmates who were wishing me well.

As I entered the front office, I encountered the warden, and he actually shook my hand and wished me good luck. He walked with me to the records office, and the records supervisor had me sign some paperwork and asked me if I had a ride.

"Yes, my sister will come and get me. Can I use a phone to call her? I will have to call her cell phone since she is at work and that number is not on my calling list."

"No problem," answered the warden.

I called April, who said that she would be here in about an hour and then rushed to my barracks to pack the small amount of property I would take with me. The rest of it, radio, headphones, and what little bit of commissary items I had in my locker box, I gave away.

When I returned to the front office, a guard took me to the property room and gave me some old clothes to wear out of prison. He then escorted me to the front gatehouse to await the arrival of my sister.

Standing outside the front entrance dressed in freeworld clothes was a rush like no drug I had ever done. It was the most wonderful feeling I have ever known. Soon after, my sister arrived; as she stepped from her mini van, I ran to her, and we hugged, me lifting her from her feet and swinging her around in a circle in celebration.

✗ ✗ ✗

"Allen! Hey, Bill, you going to work?" Somebody was pulling on my foot. "Come on, Bill. They called Outside Maintenance ten minutes ago."

"NO!" I screamed as the realization hit me that I was dreaming my release. I was not going home. The parole board and the governor had both denied my petition for clemency. I was still a convict for another nine years.

The First Good Bye

Today is Wednesday, January 7, 2004. I am still at the Tucker Unit, still a clerk at Outside Maintenance. I have remained drug and disciplinary free and am fully confident that I am a person who, if released, will never return to prison. I have learned all the necessary lessons, and the only remaining objective is to use what I have learned to help keep others from having to endure the hell I have lived.

My story didn't end on January 7, 2004. The end is still evolving. We all have to make decisions every day. It is up to each of us to shape our own future. What path do you want to follow?

The Strange Thing Is

January, Friday the 13th, 2012. I'm Free! The strange thing is, I was extradited to Arkansas from Tennessee on June, Friday the 13th, 1986 to stand trial for the Conway pharmacy robbery. Who says God does not have a sense of humor? Twenty-seven years, three months and fifteen days, including the eighteen months I did in county jails in Texas and Tennessee.

Since the time of my unsuccessful Clemency bid in the final chapter, I spent five years on the 309 Program. This is a program where trusted inmates of the Arkansas Department of Correction live at County Jails in Arkansas and are under the direct supervision of the County Sheriff. I was transferred to Ouachita County where I worked in the warrant division maintaining their database.

I left Ouachita County in March, 2010 and returned to the Tucker Unit and became enrolled in a computer course in Vo-Tech. Graduating this course I received one hundred and eighty days good time which added to the other good time I had earned for behaving myself, allowed me to discharge my fifty year prison sentence. I am not on parole and do not have to report to anyone.

The most amazing aspect of my story is not my release, it is with who I have been reunited with for the last two years. Christmas of 2009 I decided that because Speed Trap was going to be published that I needed to find and advise Debbie of this. I did some searching on the internet and thought I had found her living in Austin, Texas. I wrote her a letter telling her about the book and assuring her that I was not trying to get back into her life. I told her that if she wished to contact me she could do so at the Sheriff's Department in Ouachita County. Thirty days later it crossed my mind that Debbie must not want to contact me and I thought it was just as well, who could blame her? I had accomplished what I intended and that was to advise her of the book's publication. Later that night I got a phone call from Debbie. My search was a failure. I did not even have her correct last name and she lives in North Little Rock, Arkansas, not Austin, Texas. Debbie never received my letter, but for the last thirty days she had been unable to get me off her mind. She was even pulling my picture up on the Department of Correction web site and saying "Hello" to it/me. Finally, on January 25, 2010 she contacted my sister and asked her how to get in touch with me, and then called me.

That was two years ago and since that time Debbie never missed a week visiting me at Tucker and we were fortunate enough to spend three furloughs together. She is divorced from her husband of almost twenty-five years, has a married twenty-two year old daughter who is mother to a baby boy. Debbie and I will be remarried in April, 2012.

There is no telling how this story ends. The speed trap is a difficult one to escape. Regardless, I will never be caught within its grasp again. I have ruined my life and in the process have brought much pain to those I love and fear to the innocent victims of my robberies. I blame no one else, for the decisions have all been mine.

So, how does a person avoid the speed trap? Avoidance is easy; you simply say, "No," when asked if you want to get high. If you never take that first toke, pill, or shot, you will never have to concern yourself with being mired in the plight of drug abuse. Once you have started down the highway of getting high, it is much more difficult. I know of no "sure fire" remedy, no magical cure.

The important thing to remember is that drug abuse always starts out as drug use. After I smoked my first joint, I did not start breaking into pharmacies. I only wanted to get high. I was not hurting anybody. However, getting high on weekends turns into being stoned during the week; social toots turn into hiding in the bathroom to get loaded. Spending a few dollars a week on a buzz turns into the dope dealer getting your entire paycheck. Borrowing a little money to cop a high turns into stealing for your drugs. Stealing or dealing to support your drug habit will net you a stay in jail, and if you have not lost enough by then, a stay in the Department of Correction. If you still have not learned, the graveyards are full of people who paid the ultimate price. As for managing to get off drugs, that battle is more difficult than avoiding them. Each person is different, and I doubt many people will encounter the almost paranormal remedy I experienced. Nobody makes a decision to get off drugs unless they have paid a price. Have you lost something or someone through drug abuse? If so, and you are considering quitting, the first question you need to ask yourself is, "Have I lost enough?" If your answer is an enthusiastic, "Yes!" then I strongly suggest you enter a drug treatment program and pay close attention to the counselors, most of whom have successfully quit using drugs.

Learning how to deal with pain and how to take the knocks that life generally gives out were paramount in my successful abstinence. Every time I dealt with something that hurt me, feeling the pain and then allowing it to move on, I grew a little bit stronger. Every time life kicked me in the teeth and I did not resort to my old pattern of getting high, I gained experience. With subsequent bouts of pain or kick, I would draw upon the fact that if I had made it through last time, I can make it through this time. When the going got more than I could handle, I would pray to God to give me strength.

My only remaining hope is that one person who is either caught in the speed trap, approaching it, or finds themselves in another trap equally as deadly, will read my words and say to himself, "If he can do it, so can I! I do not want to go through what Bill went through."

One person …

Glossary

abscessed a shot   when a drug user attempts to inject a drug into a vein using a hypodermic syringe and misses and injects it into skin or muscle it causes a sore, sometime getting infected but usually going away in a few days.

Act 309 program   A program set up by the legislature and the Arkansas Department of Correction for eligible class I prisoners where the prisoners is transferred to the custody of a County Sheriff. Prisoners participating in the 309 Program work directly for the Sheriff, are usually allowed to wear civilian clothing and have much more liberty than prisoners incarcerated in prison. There are several requirements to eligibility, no rule violations in ninety days, no sex crimes, first degree or capital murder sentences, no more than ever being convicted of one aggravated robbery, and less than ten years remaining to serve on a sentence.

ADC   Arkansas Department of Correction

a dime of weed   Ten dollars worth of marijuana.

Adminseg   Administrative Segregation. Place where difficult prisoners live. Prisoners who are often committing rule violations and have a total disregard for authority are housed in a special barracks, locked in cells twenty-three hours a day.

blast off   a personal term, not a common slang. I used it when I was preparing to inject any form of amphetamine or cocaine.

building utility   job assignment for physically unfit prisoners which requires very little physical labor. Usually consists of janitorial duties.

convict   in the freeworld, refers to any person who has served time in prison. In the prisons, it refers to a person who has been tested in the prison environment and found to be strong and can be trusted by other "convicts." Prisoners were either convicts or punks. Because of the improvements made in prison security the term, left over from an earlier era when prisoners had to fight to survive, is not used much nowdays.

crank   homemade methamphetamine.

freeworld   is where non-incarcerated people live.

freeworlder   any person who is not incarcerated.

hoe squad   All physically capable new arrivals have to complete a minimum of sixty days on the hoe squad. Hoe squads work in the prison fields and are guarded by armed guards riding horses. If a person is reduced in "class" by the administration for rule violations and is physically able, is usually assigned to work on the hoe squad until he earns his class back. See: (Class I, II, II, and IV inmates)

Inmate classification is broken down into four categories, **Class I-IV. Class I**, into three categories, **Class IA, IB, & IC**. Classification determines an inmate's privileges and good time. Arkansas has several statutory variables which affect a prisoner's sentence, i.e. requirements of amount of time having to be served before parole eligibility, the amount of good time or even good time eligibility a prisoner can earn. Prison authorities can assign class in steps for good behavior or take it all away "Class IV" for rule violations.

Class I   inmates receive thirty days good time allowance each month and can have visits every Sunday.

Class IA   inmates are trustees with minimum security concerns and do not require an immediate supervisor with them when they work outside the prison fence. Usually these are just work release prisoners.**Class IB** -requires an unarmed supervisor to be with them when they are outside the fence.

Class IC   is maximum or medium security inmates.

Class II   inmates receive twenty days good time allowance each month and can have visits every other Saturday.

Class III   inmates receive ten days good time allowance each month and can have visits every other Saturday.

Class IV   inmates receive no good time or visits. Loss of class is the result of disciplinary infractions. (Breaking rules and being busted in Disciplinary Court.)

inmate   A convicted felon, generally serving a less severe sentence. Someone who adheres to the policies and rules of the prison authorities. Inmates are usually the guards biggest source of information about what other prisoners are doing.

interstate compact   offenders who are supervised by the department of corrections in any state may apply to have their supervision transferred to their "home state" with certain restrictions.

K2s   Two milligram Dilaudid pill. Dilaudid is a brand name, Hydromorphone, is the drugs name. It is a derivative of morphine, in legal terms, a narcotic. Also comes in 1, 3 and 4 milligrams. The 2 and 4 milligram strength are the ones most commonly found in a pharmacy. The reason they are called K2s and K4s in because they have a K on one side of the pill which stands for Knoll Laboratories, and a 1, 2, 3, or 4 on the other side that represents the strength in milligrams.

NCIC "National Crime Information Center. Computerized index of criminal justice information i.e. criminal record history information, fugitives, stolen properties, missing persons. It is available to Federal, state, and local law enforcement and other criminal justice agencies and is operational 24 hours a day, 365 days a year.

over-amping Shortened for "over amphetamine." Used when so much amphetamine is injected it causes the normal amphetamine effects, i.e. talking fast, accelerated heart beat, jitteriness, etc. to be reversed. Causing your heart beat to decelerate and a very strong euphoric feeling. *(See: the shot)*

papers or paperwork a term used to describe the amount of cocaine in a single-dose package for sale.

PMA Positive Mental Attitude

police, guard, officer some of the many names convicts use to refer to prison guards.

punk An inmate who allows themselves to be intimidated or forced to commit sexual act with another prisoner. The epitome of weak.

rack bed

rig hypodermic syringe and needle

sally port a secure place within the prison between the outer door and the inner part of a building.

schedule twos Any pharmaceutical drug that has the potential for abuse.

shooting dope injecting drugs with a hypodermic syringe and needle.

shooting shots injecting drugs with a hypodermic syringe and needle.

short-hair a new correctional officer

speed amphetamine pills acquired from a pharmacy. Crank sometimes is referring to homemade methamphetamine.

ten pill shot Any shot of drugs that is composed of ten pills.

the shot A personal term, not common slang. I used it when speaking or writing about an exorbitant about of amphetamine that I desired that would cause the amphetamine effects i.e., talking fast, accelerated heart beat, jitteriness, etc. to be reversed. This caused my heart beat to decelerate and a very strong euphoric feeling. Frequently relaxing even my eye muscles and causing my eyes to cross and sometimes making me pass out. *(See: over-amping)*

voir dire A preliminary examination of a witness or a juror by a judge or counsel. In context used to describe the process of choosing a jury.

Z Chevrolet Camero Z28